BIPOLAR PUZZLE SOLUTION

BIPOLAR PUZZLE SOLUTION

A Mental Health Client's Perspective

187 Answers to Questions
Asked by Support Group Members
about Living with Manic-Depressive Illness

Bryan L. Court
Gerald E. Nelson, M.D.

ACCELERATED DEVELOPMENT
A member of the Taylor & Francis Group

USA	Publishing Office:	ACCELERATED DEVELOPMENT
		A member of the Taylor & Francis Group
		1101 Vermont Avenue, N.W., Suite 200
		Washington, DC 20005-3521
		Tel: (202) 289-2174
		Fax: (202) 289-3665
	Distribution Center:	ACCELERATED DEVELOPMENT
		A member of the Taylor & Francis Group
		1900 Frost Road, Suite 101
		Bristol, PA 19007-1598
		Tel: (215) 785-5800
		Fax: (215) 785-5515
UK		Taylor & Francis Ltd.
		1 Gunpowder Square
		London EC4A 3DE
		Tel: 0171 583 0490
		Fax: 0171 583 0581

BIPOLAR PUZZLE SOLUTION: A Mental Health Client's Perspective

1 2 3 4 5 6 7 8 9 0   B R B R   9 8 7 6

This book was set in Times Roman by Sandra F. Watts. The editor was Judith L. Aymond. Technical development by Cynthia Long. Cover design by Michelle Fleitz. Printing and binding by Braun-Brumfield, Inc.

A CIP catalog record for this book is available from the British Library.
∞ The paper in this publication meets the requirements of the ANSI Standard Z39.48-1984 (Permanence of Paper)

Library of Congress Cataloging-in-Publication Data

Court, Bryan L.
    Bipolar puzzle solution : a mental health client's perspective :
187 answers to questions asked by support group members about living
with manic-depressive illness / Bryan L. Court, Gerald E. Nelson.
        p.   cm.
    Includes bibliographical references and index.

    1. Manic-depressive illness—Miscellanea.   2. Manic-depressive
illness—Popular works.   I. Nelson, Gerald E., date.
II. Title.
RC516.C68   1996
616.89'5—dc20
                                                        96-14284
                                                        CIP
    ISBN 1-56032-493-7

IN REMEMBRANCE

Of my Uncle Jim, who was very intelligent and had a lively sense of humor, who suffered through depression and other mood disturbances throughout his life without ever being correctly diagnosed and treated, who at the age of 62 took his own life in the midst of depression and despair.

B. L. C.

92828

TABLE OF CONTENTS

Note: "Q" stands for Question Number throughout this book. "PR" stands for A Psychiatrist's Response (or A Psychiatrist's Addition).

BACKGROUND
AND INTRODUCTION

In the United States, approximately one percent of the population or about 2.5 million people have a bipolar disorder (also called manic-depressive illness). These individuals have an illness that is characterized by mood cycles of depression and mania. *Bipolar Puzzle Solution* is a book that answers questions asked mostly by people with a bipolar disorder concerning their illness and how to live with it.

Those who seek help for their bipolar disorder are both the strong and courageous and the weak and fearful, but the majority of people with the illness do not seek help. Most with the illness have been misunderstood, rejected, shunned, and disliked because they had a bipolar disorder not of their own choosing. Teenagers and adults who have been depressed and suicidal, unwanted by almost everyone, through no fault of their own, are forced into a horrible existence on the streets of our country because they failed to find adequate treatment for the symptoms of their illness. Finally, there are many who suffer and search for their way out of the darkness and into the light where answers, health, freedom, hope, and love are in abundance, but there are few "road maps" for them to follow. This is reality.

For someone with a bipolar disorder, education and knowledge about the illness are necessary for successful treatment. People with the disorder, their family members, and friends listen to doctors and plow through technical books in their search for answers related to this disorder, and most would think that that was an adequate search; however, many of these same people go to support groups and ask for answers to questions not provided by their doctors or books. At support groups, the same questions are often asked several times within the same year; some never get answered. At other times, good questions are asked, and nobody readily provides a satisfactory answer. The questions that people ask about living with bipolar disorder cover a wide spectrum of subjects that include understanding the illness, treatment methods, various medications, attitudes, acceptance, faith, living problems, relationships, disability, hospitalization, and employment related difficulties. Some of these areas fall outside the expertise of the physician, and the physician is unable to answer them all.

Most people with the illness feel lost while trying to get answers because they do not know where to look. Others give up after an unsuccessful attempt to find a clear, concise answer from a thick, complex, technical book written with words that only a psychiatrist understands. People want a better, easier way to guide themselves through the educational component of recovery than the current method of letting them find their own way through the maze of living with bipolar illness. The solution lies in providing simple, clear answers in one location to most of the questions asked about bipolar illness by the average patient, friend, and family member.

Over a period of many months, all the questions that were asked in one particular bipolar support group were written down. Other relevant questions that were expressed in other types of support groups also were recorded. Having all these questions answered in book form would be helpful to those who had questions about living with bipolar disorder. If a person could get answers to common questions all at once, their understanding of recovery would be speeded up and enhanced. Much time and money would be saved by this compilation because mental health professionals would not be spending time explaining the basics already discussed in the book. Finally, until now, no single book has been on the market in any form that answers the wide range of questions. In *Bipolar Puzzle Solution,* 187 questions over the broad range of interest to the patient, family, and friend are addressed specifically.

Bipolar Puzzle Solution was written with the same question and answer conversational format heard in bipolar support groups rather than a standard textbook format, and the majority of "pieces" that compose the "bipolar puzzle" have come together in this unique arrangement. Many books about bipolar disorders have been written with a doctor's perspective, but this book is meant to give the rarer perspective of someone with the illness.

Those seeking to learn about living problems associated with bipolar disorders readily identify with sound material written by a patient and prefer it.

The answers contained in this book represent the opinions, concerns, and experience heard from others with bipolar illness in a support group setting. Some of the answers were obtained from psychiatrists, a labor law attorney, hospital employees, and various books and publications. My current psychiatrist, Gerald E. Nelson, M.D., reviewed the answers to the questions and provided a response to most sections of this book. This process yielded a relevant, accurate, complete, and easily understood information source.

Bryan L. Court

A PSYCHIATRIST'S COMMENTS

Bipolar disorder or manic-depressive illness now is recognized far more frequently at its earlier, more subtle stages than when I graduated from medical school 36 years ago. I first practiced in a small farm community in rural Minnesota for 10 years, and I know I did not recognize the vast majority of patients with complaints suggestive of bipolar disorder. I only recognized those few who demonstrated the more extreme forms of the illness and referred them for psychiatric treatment.

I have been a psychiatrist for over 20 years, and each year I see more patients whose symptoms conform to the diagnosis of bipolar disorder. The signs and symptoms may be vague and subtle but, with careful investigation of the patient's history (especially the family history) plus a careful physical examination, a diagnosis may be made and appropriate treatment initiated.

I also consider bipolar illness as a diagnosis for children (ages 8 to 18) because a significant number of children with a diagnosis of attention deficit disorder (ADD) actually are suffering from the early stages of bipolar disorder.

If the subtle signs and symptoms of bipolar disorder are recognized early, before a devastating breakdown, treatment is likely to be much more successful with much less loss and devastation. I have had the opportunity to follow patients for many years as they struggle with the many attributes of bipolar disorder. This has caused me to gain a certain amount of humility and patience, and I am much more optimistic about the outcome of treatment in children, teenagers, and adults. I know that disorders can be serious and devastating, and they can ruin individuals and their families; however, I do not believe this is necessary. From my many years of following children, teenagers, and adults over the course of their illness, I have come to be quite optimistic about our ability to respond to the patient as a physician, family, friend, or community.

So it was with great interest and anticipation that I waited for Bryan to complete his collection of questions and responses to them. This process took over a year as he persisted and wrestled with questions, concepts, ideas, and interacted with different professionals. I reviewed the questions and responses in this book and found them to be relevant, easy to understand, and the answers to be complete and accurate. I intend to give this book to every patient or parent of a patient who has bipolar disorder because education, self-knowledge, and knowledge about the person with the illness are vital to successful treatment.

Gerald E. Nelson, M.D.

Hope . . .

For every small box,
     a lid waits to be removed.

For every confining room,
     a door leads to freedom.

For every dark night,
     a day of brightness will follow.

For every complex problem,
     an answer can be found with effort.

For every horrible nightmare,
     an end is certain.

For every type of puzzle,
     a solution lives and waits for discovery.

Bryan L. Court

BRYAN'S INTRODUCTION TO THE ILLNESS

My bipolar disorder started with a rude surprise as my first episode of depression came rapidly out of nowhere when I was 20 years old. A nine-and-a-half-year period began that included scattered periods of depression lasting from a few weeks to several months. I graduated from college and was able to work full-time, but some periods of time were very difficult due to depression. Because of the conversations, statements, and opinions relating to psychiatrists and their profession that I had heard while growing up, I did not trust them. I actually thought they would do me more harm than good. Medications frightened me, and I avoided people who prescribed them; I didn't want to become addicted and have another problem. I was ignorant of the truth surrounding my illness, and that kept me from seeking help.

By the age of 24, a new symptom of racing thoughts occurring for several days at a time had emerged, and stopping the thoughts was difficult or impossible. Weeks of depression, days with racing thoughts, and varying lengths of time in a neutral mood were standard for me. One of my depressions was worse than I had ever experienced. I finally saw a psychiatrist; however, my visits over the following three years didn't give me much relief. I attended 12-step groups that helped me a great deal, but they did not cure me of manic-depressive symptoms. My friends were disgusted with me, and they always told me things that I had failed to do that had caused my depression. I didn't believe that my friends knew what they were talking about. My self-esteem, self-confidence, and faith gradually were eroded by all the criticism of well-intentioned

1

individuals. I was very disillusioned and believed that there was no relief for my symptoms. I felt lost and incapable of managing my emotions.

In my late-20s, the hypomanic part of my illness (my "hyper" part) got worse. My brain felt as if it were being overworked at times, and I believed that I would have a short life because I felt so miserable. My work hours were cut in half because I was always tired, and in-depth thinking was difficult. At times, I was scared because I thought there was no solution. Everyday, death seemed preferable to a lifetime of these severe symptoms. Summoning the will to go on was a daily chore.

When I was almost 30 years old, I volunteered a few hours per week toward helping teenagers, and one of them had similar symptoms as I had. Eventually, that young man was hospitalized and diagnosed with bipolar disorder. I had symptoms just like his, and this made me think I had the same illness. The cyclical nature of my moods over the years was obvious to me, and I charted or graphed the "hyper" and depressive extremes to prove to myself and others that my moods were going up and down. Shortly afterwards, I went to a new psychiatrist who immediately diagnosed me with bipolar illness; the graph I made proved an invaluable aid in the diagnostic process. Within a month, I started medication. Several weeks later, my symptoms vanished, and I discovered that relief from the symptoms was as simple as taking medication.

In the months that followed, I had difficulty reversing the embedded belief that my mood swings were my fault. I doubted that I really had the illness because I compared myself to TV and movie characters. Their extreme expression of bipolar disorder wasn't like mine; therefore, I doubted that I had the illness. I spent much time blaming myself for the inability to "snap out of it," and I wondered if my symptoms were really caused by a biochemical problem. What was right? What was true? Was I really mentally ill? Many questions went through my mind, and I needed and wanted answers; some of these follow. What is this thing (illness) that has a hold on me? Did I cause it? How can I change it? How common is this illness? Would I be the same person after medication? Where can I go to get answers to my questions? Whom should I tell? Whom do I trust? Who are my friends? How will bipolar illness change me and the rest of my life? Am I flawed? Am I as good as I used to be? How do I stop feeling so ignorant about my life-dominating illness?

It has been more than 17 years since my illness began, and I have learned that my illness is called Bipolar-II Disorder. The symptoms of my illness have been successfully treated with medication for the last seven years, and I don't have any more episodes of depression or hypomania. Also, I feel very fortunate that I don't have any partial symptoms remaining. After the symptoms of my illness went away, I slowly worked my way back to full-time employment.

Initially, I spent a great deal of time educating myself, my family, and my friends about the illness, and this still continues today but at a lower priority. Through the process of talking to relatives, I discovered that there was a history of this illness in my family. The actions and behaviors of relatives began to make sense as I began to see the illness in relatives. Now with most of the educational process behind me, my only complaint is that I don't like some of the side effects of my medication; however, I can live with that considering the alternatives. Overall, I am very grateful because I have found an adequate solution to my "bipolar puzzle," and with this understanding have come peace and acceptance.

In my own life, I have discovered that nothing can replace my own efforts in the recovery process. I found that I had to try with great effort every day to find answers to my life. My recovery didn't just happen; it was work.

Many of the answers to questions in this book require an effort to complete, whereas others are just the outline of a process that the reader is urged to follow. Doctors can give us a lot of help, guidance, and encouragement, but they are neither able nor willing to do every required task for us in our recovery. Much of the recovery process is left for us to pursue, and the pursuit of answers and solutions takes a great deal of time, energy, effort, and patience on our part.

I wish you the best in your effort to find answers, and remember, you'll get out of it what you put into it.

PR-1. A PSYCHIATRIST'S RESPONSE

Bryan's description of his illness is typical of the history that many patients give when they seek help for their manic-depressive illness. Bryan's history is fairly typical in its onset, his lack of response to psychotherapy alone, and his excellent response to lithium.

This disorder was first accurately described in the second century by a Greek physician, and it has been described through the ensuing centuries in a number of different ways although the basic signs and symptoms remain unchanged. Even to this date, debate and discussion continue about the causes of the illness and how to categorize and treat the different variations of the manic-depressive disorder.

The mental health community now, however, feels relatively confident in its ability to diagnose and treat the vast majority of patients with bipolar disorder, including those who exhibit subtle and mild symptoms. Even children (ages 8 to 18) now are diagnosed as having bipolar disorder and are successfully treated before the illness causes serious impairment and loss.

A contemporary primary care physician or a mental health professional would be quite likely to have spotted Bryan's symptoms, considered a diagnosis of bipolar disorder, and either started him on a medication program or referred him to a psychiatrist trained and experienced in treating bipolar disorder.

Bryan has made an excellent accommodation and adaptation to his illness. His family remains understanding, supportive, and open to any new information Bryan gives them. He is a member of several groups that provide him further knowledge, information, and support. His friends have accepted the changes wrought by his illness, and, most of all, Bryan has fully integrated the illness, the effects of treatment, and responses of family, friends, and employer so that he is a source of information and wisdom for me as one of his treating psychiatrists.

This book was part of Bryan's treatment program. Bryan's intelligence and hard work were put to good use while focusing on the scope of and variety within bipolar illness to produce a book of unusual usefulness.

THE ILLNESS

Q-1. Briefly, what is manic-depressive illness (or bipolar disorder)?

Let me preface my response with a short definition for several words used therein.

mood: an all-encompassing and persistent emotion that influences one's outlook on life.

mania: a mood disorder characterized by excessive euphoria, hyperactivity, restlessness, and accelerated thoughts and speech.

depression: a mood characterized by sadness, despair, hopelessness, guilt, discouragement, slowed thinking, lowered energy, and decreased pleasure.

normal: a neutral, peaceful, relaxed state that people associate with feeling normal.

Manic-depressive illness is a mood disorder of *biological origins,* and a person with this illness has mood changes back and forth from mania to depression usually interspersed with periods of normal moods.

Q-2. What classifies or diagnoses me as having manic-depressive illness (or bipolar disorder)?

Because a physical test (e.g., a blood test) for bipolar disorder is not available on the market, a doctor has only our history (i.e., as we see it and our family sees it), our behavior, and our current moods to use to evaluate and make a diagnosis. If you have a previous illness history from another doctor and your family medical history, they also are needed. It is important to look into your own past and make a record of how you felt, your behavior, and how long you had manic and/or depressive symptoms. If this illness is just beginning, it may take a while longer to get an accurate diagnosis because some history of the illness is necessary.

The diagnostic criteria for this illness is specified in the American Psychiatric Association's *Diagnostic and Statistical Manual of Mental Disorders, Fourth Edition* (1994), also referred to as the DSM-IV. Essentially, **Bipolar-I Disorder** includes a history of one or more Manic Episodes usually with one or more Major Depressive Episodes. **Bipolar-II Disorder** includes Hypomanic Episodes and Major Depressive Episodes. Another form of bipolar illness is called **cyclothymia,** which includes numerous Hypomanic Episodes and numerous periods with depressive symptoms (rather than Major Depressive Episodes). A Bipolar Disorder, Mixed Episode, includes Manic and Major Depressive Episodes intermixed nearly every day for at least one week. (See Q-4 for a description of a Manic Episode, Q-6 for a Hypomanic Episode, and Q-10 for a Major Depressive Episode.)

Q-3. Why are there two names for this illness?

Although the terms manic or mania and depressive or depression still are used to describe the two mood extremes, the phrase manic-depressive is old terminology. The illness is known today in medical terms as bipolar disorder or bipolar affective disorder. The disorder is named or called bipolar in the DSM-IV rather than manic-depressive.

Q-4. What are the symptoms of mania?

The intensity of manic symptoms varies from mild to serious impairment and can develop completely within a few days. Mania can last as long as several months unless it is treated. Symptoms of mania are extreme for the individual given the situation in which they are felt and the individual's normal personality. The manic behavior is out of both proportion and character to what is really happening in and around the person.

The list below (A-E) contains the diagnostic criteria for a Manic Episode from the DSM-IV (American Psychiatric Association, 1994, p. 332). I have added some definitions to a few words found in the DSM-IV description of a Manic Episode; my definitions are enclosed in brackets.

Criteria for Manic Episode

A. A distinct period of abnormally and persistently elevated, expansive, or irritable mood, lasting at least 1 week (or any duration if hospitalization is necessary).
B. During the period of mood disturbance, three (or more) of the following symptoms have persisted (four if the mood is only irritable) and have been present to a significant degree:

   (1) inflated self-esteem or grandiosity
   (2) decreased need for sleep (e.g., feels rested after only 3 hours of sleep)
   (3) more talkative than usual or pressure to keep talking
   (4) flight of ideas or subjective experience that thoughts are racing [*Flight of ideas* is almost a continuous flow of rapid speech (or thought) that jumps from topic to topic with each new topic usually related to the previous topic. In severe cases, the rapid speech may be disorganized and incoherent.]
   (5) distractibility (i.e., attention too easily drawn to unimportant or irrelevant external stimuli)
   (6) increase in goal-directed activity (either socially, at work or school, or sexually) or psychomotor agitation [*Psychomotor agitation* is a generalized physical expression of rapid thought and is based on something going on in the mind rather than an organic disease. Some examples are restless movement of the hands, legs, or feet, or pacing back and forth.]
   (7) excessive involvement in pleasurable activities that have a high potential for painful consequences (e.g., engaging in unrestrained buying sprees, sexual indiscretions, or foolish business investments)

C. The symptoms do not meet criteria for a Mixed Episode. (See DSM-IV, American Psychiatric Association, 1994, p. 335.)
D. The mood disturbance is sufficiently severe to cause marked impairment in occupational functioning or in usual social activities or relationships with others, or to necessitate hospitalization to prevent harm to self or others, or there are psychotic features.
E. The symptoms are not due to the direct physiological effects of a substance (e.g., a drug of abuse, a medication, or other treatment) or a general medical condition (e.g., hyperthyroidism).

Note: Manic-like episodes that are clearly caused by somatic antidepressant treatment (e.g., medication, electroconvulsive therapy, light therapy) should not count toward a diagnosis of Bipolar I Disorder.

The following list (1-14) is a short compilation of mania descriptions from individuals at my support group, but they're not for official diagnostic purposes.

1. Feeling overly important or powerful.
2. Feelings of expansiveness characterized by richness, abundance, magnificence, or excessive goodness.
3. Feelings of "being on top of the world", unwarranted optimism.
4. Feelings of exhilaration, elation, thrill, or delight beyond normal.
5. Talking rapidly and continuously. May not make sense.
6. Being irritable, oversensitive, and testy.
7. Being impatient, overly eager, restless.
8. Eating little.
9. Having racing thoughts that cannot be stopped.
10. Impaired or poor judgement resulting in some dangerous situations.
11. Acting without regard to consequence.
12. Acting impulsively, spontaneously, and unpredictably.
13. Cannot sit still.
14. Jumping from one project to another, never completing anything.

Q-5. Can someone have manic episodes without ever having depressive periods?

Yes. Although they represent a minority within the spectrum of bipolar illness, some are essentially unipolar manic but are officially classified as having bipolar disorder. They cycle from a normal mood state to mania and back without having a depressive episode.

Q-6. What is *hypomania*? Describe it.

Hypomania is a lesser form of mania; "hypo" means lower. The symptoms are the same as for mania (see Q-4), but they are less intense. The list below (A-F) contains the diagnostic criteria for a Hypomanic Episode from the DSM-IV (American Psychiatric Association, 1994, p. 338).

Criteria for Hypomanic Episode

A. A distinct period of persistently elevated, expansive, or irritable mood, lasting throughout at least 4 days, that is clearly different from the usual non-depressed mood.

B. During the period of mood disturbance, three (or more) of the following symptoms have persisted (four if the mood is only irritable) and have been present to a significant degree:

(1) inflated self-esteem or grandiosity
(2) decreased need for sleep (e.g., feels rested after only 3 hours of sleep)
(3) more talkative than usual or pressure to keep talking
(4) flight of ideas or subjective experience that thoughts are racing
(5) distractibility (i.e., attention too easily drawn to unimportant or irrelevant external stimuli)
(6) increase in goal-directed activity (either socially, at work or school, or sexually) or psychomotor agitation
(7) excessive involvement in pleasurable activities that have a high potential for painful consequences (e.g., the person engages in unrestrained buying sprees, sexual indiscretions, or foolish business investments)

C. The episode is associated with an unequivocal change in functioning that is uncharacteristic of the person when not symptomatic.
D. The disturbance in mood and the change in functioning are observable by others.
E. The episode is not severe enough to cause marked impairment in social or occupational functioning, or to necessitate hospitalization, and there are no psychotic features.
F. The symptoms are not due to the direct physiological effects of a substance (e.g., a drug of abuse, a medication, or other treatment) or a general medical condition (e.g., hyperthyroidism).

Note: Hypomanic-like episodes that are clearly caused by somatic antidepressant treatment (e.g., medication, electroconvulsive therapy, light therapy) should not count toward a diagnosis of Bipolar II Disorder.

When I was hypomanic, I could not stop the thoughts that raced through my mind. I had many symptoms of mania, but they were mild and not incapacitating. I felt as if my mind was going fast, and my attempts to slow it down failed. I drove around in my car for hours and loved the movement of the car and visual stimulation as I listened to fast-paced music on my car stereo. I always thought others talked too slowly, and I was always ready for a rapid stream of information. The world went too slowly for me! At other times, I had a tired, pressurized feeling in my head as if I had studied all day or taken an 8-hour exam. I described my brain as having a burning sensation around the edges. Also, I could "hear" a constant hissing noise and felt as if my brain or mind was overworked. I believed that it was working hard at all levels in addition to the conscious level. After a couple days of these symptoms, I became concerned because I wasn't getting enough sleep, and then I stopped liking the hypomanic episode.

Q-7. Why are mania and hypomania so difficult for my doctor to diagnose?

Diagnosing mania and hypomania can be difficult because these moods must coincide with a doctor's visit. Extreme mania is easily recognized by your doctor, but it may end before you get to the doctor, depending on the time interval between appointments. If you are seeing a doctor for the first time, you may appear to be energized naturally rather than hypomanically. Hypomania can be disguised even from a psychiatrist in many cases, but some doctors are better tuned to spotting hypomania than others.

In the first three years that I saw a psychiatrist, he recognized only the severe depressive periods that I had. I gave him symptoms of hypomania not knowing what they were. I acted "perfectly normal" in the doctor's office, and he never diagnosed me as hypomanic or having bipolar disorder. He said if I couldn't sleep or had the symptoms I described, I should take a few Extra-Strength Tylenol. The Tylenol took away some of the symptoms, and I was able to sleep for three to four hours at a time. Then I would take two more Tylenol and go back to sleep. Because my doctor didn't diagnose me accurately, I took thousands of Tylenol over a period of six years.

Twice a week for three years, I uselessly spent a great deal of time and money in psychotherapy for a biological problem. My doctor always asked me whether I was angry towards my mother or father while trying to get at the supposed psychological root of my depression. We worked successfully on many other emotional and psychological issues, but my major problems with depression and hypomania persisted. I finally stopped seeing him and didn't go back to another psychiatrist for two and a half years; I wrongly concluded that the solution to my depression and hypomania wasn't with doctors.

Q-8. How do I know if I'm hypomanic or just "hyper"?

First, read the requirements for a Hypomanic Episode in Q-6, and read over the descriptions of mania. If you have no hypomanic symptoms, you are just "hyper." If you have some hypomanic symptoms, try to end them by turning them off or trying to stop them. If you can stop them, you are just "hyper." If you have very little or no control over your symptoms, you are hypomanic.

Q-9. Is rage or anger a part of this illness?

An irritable mood is common in mania and hypomania. Sudden rage usually occurs when a person's "great" plans are ruined. I also have heard people describe the angry outbursts and rages that they have while hypomanic or manic; sometimes anger is the most noticeable symptom of their hypomanic or manic episode. When I was either depressed or hypomanic, part of my anger came from frustration over my attempts to get help with the illness, and my irritable mood was a base on which to build anger. An irritable mood also can be present in the depressive phase of the illness.

Irritability can be difficult to manage or control. Here are three things you can do that might help: (a) step back and recognize your irritability, (b) take time out from whatever you are doing, and (c) decrease sensory input, especially sound.

Q-10. What are the symptoms of depression?

The first list below (A-E) contains the diagnostic criteria for a Major Depressive Episode from DSM-IV (American Psychiatric Association, 1994, p. 327). The intensity of depressive symptoms varies from mild to serious impairment and can develop completely within a few days; for some, depression can last more than a year or two unless it is treated.

Criteria for Major Depressive Episode

A. Five (or more) of the following symptoms have been present during the same 2-week period and represent a change from previous functioning; at least one of the symptoms is either (1) depressed mood or (2) loss of interest or pleasure.

   Note: Do not include symptoms that are clearly due to a general medical condition, or mood-incongruent delusions or hallucinations.

   (1) depressed mood most of the day, nearly every day, as indicated by either subjective report (e.g., feels sad or empty) or observation made by others (e.g., appears tearful). **Note:** In children and adolescents, can be irritable mood.
   (2) markedly diminished interest or pleasure in all, or almost all, activities most of the day, nearly every day (as indicated by either subjective account or observation made by others)

(3) significant weight loss when not dieting or weight gain (e.g., a change of more than 5% of body weight in a month), or decrease or increase in appetite nearly every day. **Note**: In children, consider failure to make expected weight gains.

(4) insomnia or hypersomnia nearly every day

(5) psychomotor agitation or retardation nearly every day (observable by others, not merely subjective feelings of restlessness or being slowed down)

(6) fatigue or loss of energy nearly every day

(7) feelings of worthlessness or excessive or inappropriate guilt (which may be delusional) nearly every day (not merely self-reproach or guilt about being sick)

(8) diminished ability to think or concentrate, or indecisiveness, nearly every day (either by subjective account or as observed by others)

(9) recurrent thoughts of death (not just fear of dying), recurrent suicidal ideation without a specific plan, or a suicide attempt or a specific plan for committing suicide

B. The symptoms do not meet criteria for a Mixed Episode. (See DSM-IV, American Psychiatric Association, 1994, p. 335.)

C. The symptoms cause clinically significant distress or impairment in social, occupational, or other important areas of functioning.

D. The symptoms are not due to the direct physiological effects of a substance (e.g., a drug of abuse, a medication) or a general medical condition (e.g., hypothyroidism).

E. The symptoms are not better accounted for by Bereavement, i.e., after the loss of a loved one, the symptoms persist for longer than 2 months or are characterized by marked functional impairment, morbid preoccupation with worthlessness, suicidal ideation, psychotic symptoms, or psychomotor retardation.

The following second list (1-14) is a short compilation of depression descriptions from individuals at my support group, but they're not intended for official diagnostic purposes.

1. Feeling sad, unhappy, dejected, hopeless, worthless, and/or dismal.
2. Feelings of sluggishness, fatigue, and lethargy.
3. Worrying more than normal.
4. Lack of concentration while doing daily tasks.
5. Slow thought processes.
6. Decreased interest in friends, hobbies, and activities.

7. Inability to have "fun" doing things.
8. Seeing the world as a dark, lonely place as if the world was seen through a shadow.
9. Wanting to isolate and insulate oneself from social contact.
10. Being bored with a feeling of inner deadness where nothing at all is interesting.
11. Having vivid dreams of being so evil and rotten that others and the environment are attempting to destroy you.
12. Identification with dark colors such as black, and navy blue.
13. Having morbid suicidal thoughts, imaginations, or fantasies.
14. Suicide attempts.

Q-11. Is anxiety common in severe depression?

Yes. For many people with severe depression, coexisting anxiety is common. For example, when I was severely depressed for several weeks in 1982, I was also in a constant state of extreme anxiety. Subconsciously, I was frightened and anxious over how bad I felt from depression. Nothing that I tried doing would relax me. I could hardly eat anything, and my heart was beating faster than normal because I was so overwhelmed with anxiety. I remember seeing a bright red azalea bush, so bright and intense that my senses were extremely stimulated and my anxiety increased. My panic over a bright red flower showed how extreme my anxiety was. After several weeks of seeing a psychiatrist, my depression began to lift; as depression vanished, so did the anxiety.

Q-12. Can depression kill me?

Not directly. Depression, however, can distort your thoughts and put you in a suicidal mood, and you could choose to kill yourself. Depression can take away your appetite so that you don't eat and, consequently, you could die from a lack of nutrition. If you try to medicate your depression, you could die from an overdose of those drugs. Thus, if you make wrong choices concerning the treatment of depression, you could kill yourself in the process. With today's cures for the symptoms of depression, you do not have to stay depressed. Those who choose to seek professional help get better!

Q-13. How many people have bipolar disorder?

The statistics vary from study to study, but the percentage of the population with bipolar illness is thought to be from 0.4% to 1.2%. From the books that I have read, I believe that the actual percentage of the population that will develop this disorder sometime in their lives is closer to 1.0% or 1.2% percent. This range includes both Bipolar-I *and* Bipolar-II disorders.

Q-14. In terms of percentage, are men as susceptible as women to bipolar illness?

The odds of having this illness in a lifetime are about equal for men and women.

Q-15. Does the occurrence of this disorder vary with race?

No. Bipolar disorder affects all races approximately the same. Cultural variances may disguise or hide the symptoms and make diagnosis more difficult, but the illness is thought to transcend cultures and races.

Q-16. Can someone easily see that bipolar disorder runs in their family?

I have talked with many who have family members and relatives with this illness. Some families have named the illness and, in my case, our family called it the "Family Temper." I often would hear my grandmother say, "you have the Family Temper." A few individuals, however, have no known relatives with the illness.

Obtaining family history of this illness from older family members is difficult. In "older days," family members called people with bipolar disorder crazy or said they "had a loose screw." Some unintentionally hid their illness by drinking excessively and were known for drinking too much rather than having the illness. Others ran off for months because of mania, and no relatives were able to see their illness. A relative who had bipolar disorder may have been incarcerated for committing a crime and was labeled "the black sheep" of the family. Relatives may have shut the memory of this illness out of their minds because it was an embarrassment. Finally, older relatives probably didn't (or don't) have the vocabulary or terminology to describe this illness adequately.

Q-17. Is the cause of this illness genetic or environmental?

There is strong evidence that bipolar disorder is genetic or hereditary in many with the illness. Genetic researchers believe that they have located at least one spot on a gene that makes some people susceptible to bipolar disorder. The illness actually may be caused by one or more defective genes, but the *exact* method of passing on this defect to others is unknown. Studies of identical twins reveal that, if one twin has the illness, the other has a much higher probability of getting the illness than the general population. In some families, however, there is only one person with the illness and no hereditary pattern.

The environment plays a secondary role in many with bipolar disorder by providing the stressful events necessary to initiate some manic or depressive periods.

Q-18. What is the likelihood of passing bipolar disorder on to my child?

If one parent has the illness, a child has nearly a 30% risk of having a mood disorder (also called affective disorder) such as depression or bipolar disorder. If both parents have the illness, a child has approximately a 75% risk of developing a mood disorder.

In my case, bipolar illness is easily seen for several generations on my mother's side of the family. Although I developed bipolar illness through my mother, *she* never developed any symptoms of the illness and is now 58 years of age. Thus, a parent can remain symptom-free and have children who later develop the illness.

The majority of people with bipolar disorder have a relative with some form of mood disorder. Blood-related relatives are 10 to 20 times more likely to develop either depression or bipolar disorder than the general population.

Q-19. When does this illness usually start?

This illness begins in the late-teens or early twenties more frequently than in any other age group with a median age of onset (beginning of illness) in the early or mid-20s. (Median means there are as many people with onset over the median as below it.) Determining this median age of onset has been difficult because ages at the first treatment and first hospitalization may have been reported as the age of first symptoms, and these numbers would cause the median age to appear higher than it actually is.

Some cases have been reported as young as age 10, but cases earlier than puberty are a controversial. Often a diagnosis is difficult for an adolescent (teenager) because symptoms associated with antisocial behavior, moodiness, or drug use cause confusion in diagnosis and mimic symptoms of the illness. As a person ages beyond the late-20s, the likelihood of first onset begins to drop off significantly. Although infrequent, first onset with bipolar disorder can occur past age 60.

Q-20. Do most cases of bipolar illness start with a manic episode or a depressive episode?

Estimates of the percentage of those who begin with a manic episode vary widely, but a slight majority begin with mania.

My first episode was depressive. I have written a summary of that experience entitled "The Light at the End of the Tunnel." Look for it after the last question, Q-187.

Q-21. What is *psychosis*?

My definition of a psychotic individual says that the individual believes, perceives, or senses something that is real, in part or in whole, only to that person. A person who has psychosis is called psychotic, and a minority of individuals with bipolar disorder experience psychotic episodes. As an example of psychosis, I know a young man who believed that "a blue laser beam could come out of his finger at will, and that he could 'zap' birds with it." On another occasion, I found him after he had been in a fight while defending his claims to be Jesus Christ. He was very serious about both of these beliefs.

For a person with a history of psychosis, changes in sleep, energy, and concentration are the indicators that a psychotic period is coming up. Next, changes in thought processes occur, and these may include thought insertion, thought withdrawal, thought blocking, and thought disorganization. A person may have thoughts or beliefs that have no basis in reality, and sometimes follow no logical sequence. Some perceive things or events as clues to a great puzzle that they follow in search of the end. Psychotic people also can "see things," "hear voices" and other sounds, smell differently, and feel things such as imagined bugs crawling on them or other tactile sensations. The period of time that a person experiences psychosis is called a psychotic episode, which can range in duration from hours to days. During a psychotic episode, the person may be frightened and aware of the altered perceptions but not be able to stop them. Also, their sense of reality is diminished or absent, and they may not know what they did during that period of time. The spectrum of psychotic symptoms varies significantly from very few to many and can occur both in manic and depressive episodes.

Q-22. Is bipolar disorder a personality disorder?

No. Bipolar disorder is separate and distinct from a personality disorder, but a person with a bipolar disorder can have a personality disorder in addition to bipolar illness.

I have listed the types of personality disorders so that you can recognize them if you see them again, but adequate definitions are beyond the scope of this book. If you have been diagnosed with a personality disorder, I suggest doing some in-depth research for your own satisfaction and peace of mind. Personality disorders have been grouped into three clusters: (a) *paranoid, schizoid,* and *schizotypal*; (b) *histrionic, narcissistic, antisocial,* and *borderline*; and (c) *avoidant, dependent, compulsive,* and *passive-aggressive.*

Q-23. I have bipolar disorder. Does that mean I am crazy?

Crazy is a cruel word meant to label, stigmatize, categorize, and judge someone who happens to be mentally ill. Most people with bipolar disorder perceive the word "crazy" as offensive, and it has no place in our times describing a serious medical illness. The word only serves to frighten people away from those who are lonely and hurting. More appropriate questions might be: Am I manic? Am I depressed? Or perhaps, am I psychotic?

Q-24. Am I mentally ill?

You have a mental illness, but you are not mentally ill. The word "you" encompasses all your thoughts and emotions as well as your body and spirit. The statement that "you are mentally ill" implies that everything that defines you is mentally ill. You are a very complex, average human being who just happens to have a bipolar disorder (or a mental illness). The phrase "you are mentally ill" puts you in a category much different from the rest of society. It is much easier and more accurate for you to believe that you are quite normal in every respect except that you have a mood disorder.

Bipolar disorder is listed in a diagnostic book of mental disorders as a mental illness. Many find this difficult to accept because mental illness has been regarded as a moral weakness by society; however, one of the latest preferred ways to view this illness is to call it a *neurobiological disorder* or a *medical illness* or *condition* adversely affected by psychological factors.

In truth, your brain isn't functioning correctly in one small area affecting moods, and that causes bipolar illness. On the other hand, your brain probably is working quite well at doing the majority of required tasks, and this part of your brain isn't mentally ill. Once you are treated adequately, you still have this medical illness, but you should have few, if any, symptoms. Calling it a medical condition, or neurobiological disorder, rather than a mental illness removes stigma, puts the illness in its proper place, and encourages people to get treatment.

Q-25. What is cycling?

Cycling is the word used to describe the process of going from depression to mania and back or vice versa. These cycles can be as short as a few days to as long as months or years.

Q-26. What is a rapid cycler?

A *rapid cycler* is a person who has four or more manic, hypomanic, or depressive episodes in any twelve-month period. In extreme cases, rapid cyclers can change from depression to mania and back or vice versa in as short as a few days without a normal mood period between episodes. Although these shorter periods don't meet the time requirements for full episodes, they still are considered episodes. For more quick information on this subject, read *In Bipolar Illness: Rapid Cycling & Its Treatment* (National Depressive and Manic-Depressive Association, 1991). Also, see Q-96 for a related question on rapid cycling.

Q-27. Is there a way to keep track of my "ups" and "downs"?

Before a doctor diagnosed me with bipolar disorder, I noticed that I periodically went from being depressed to being "hyper" and back to depressed. I clearly saw the cycles in my moods. To better understand them, I *charted* my moods on a graph for about three months. The bottom part of the graph represented days, and the numbers on the left side were numerical ratings for my mood. Also, I commented with one or two words on the graph when I felt or experienced an unusual or significant symptom. With this graph in hand, not knowing what kind of a doctor to see, I went to a psychologist. He said that because this was a biological disorder, I did not need counseling. He then gave me the name of a psychiatrist. The psychiatrist reviewed my graphs and said that I had bipolar disorder.

If a doctor asks us to give our mood history over the last several months, we probably would come up with generalities. A daily graph speaks much more clearly.

Q-28. I have heard that charting or graphing my moods is a helpful tool in understanding my illness. How can I make a graph?

The rating scale shown in Figure 2.1 is a composite from one that I saw a few years ago in a support group (author unknown) and my own version created just before I was diagnosed in 1987. The positive ratings indicate mania and hypomania, while the negative ratings indicate depression. The +5 through –5 ratings go on the left-hand side (y-axis) of a graph (see Figure 2.2); these ratings are described in the Depression-Mania Ratings Scale shown in Figure 2.1. If you feel that your moods are between two of these ratings, give yourself a rating in the middle (a half point between). The bottom part (x-axis) (see Figure 2.2) is for time and can indicate 24-hour periods or even 12-hour periods. I suggest using the 12-hour periods because you can record the way you feel in the morning and at night. At each time point on the graph, plot the numerical rating that best describes your mood. Use graph paper (4 or 5 squares/inch) for your graph and connect all your ratings to form a mood line. Keep track of your moods for as long as necessary to establish your characteristic pattern; several months was enough for me.

Figure 2.2 is an example of a mood ratings graph with depression and mania ratings plotted. In this example, the ratings are plotted in 24-hour intervals, but you might want to plot them every 12 hours. On my graphs, I used the color blue to draw the mood line for depression and red to draw the mood line for mania. For a clearer view of how much time and depth you spend depressed relative to the time and depth spent manic, you could shade in the area between the mood line and the zero mood line with different colors (like blue and red) for depression and mania. For example, if the color blue (depression) was predominant on the graph, depression would be shown as more common than mania.

Q-29. Is creativity higher in people with bipolar illness than in the general population?

Yes. A higher percentage of creative people have bipolar disorder than the rest of the population. People with bipolar disorder have been among artists, novelists, playwrights, poets, political leaders, and religious leaders to name a few. Here are some who appear from historical accounts to have had some form of bipolar disorder: Alexander the Great, Napoleon Bonaparte, Winston Churchill, Oliver Cromwell, Ralph Waldo Emerson, F. Scott Fitzgerald, Vincent van Gogh, Alexander Hamilton, Ernest Hemingway, Abraham Lincoln, Martin Luther, Herman Melville, Benito Mussolini, Lord Nelson, Edgar Allan Poe, and Theodore Roosevelt. Of course, these individuals didn't have a modern physi-

Depression-Mania Ratings Scale

+5   Extremely active all the time, should be hospitalized to prevent exhaustion and consequences of bad decisions and irresponsible behavior, mostly out of control, very little sleep likely. Hypomania cannot have a +5 rating.

+4   Unable to slow down behavior and thoughts with much effort, impaired judgment possible, irresponsible actions are common, bordering on being out of control, much less sleep needed (more than 2 hours less than usual). This is maximum rating for hypomania.

+3   Overly active physically and mentally, difficult to slow down behavior and thoughts, 1 to 2 hours less sleep needed.

+2   Very energetic and active physically and mentally but not out of control, ½ to 1 hour less sleep needed.

+1   More active than normal, more energy than normal, may be more productive than normal.

 0   Normal, tranquil mood; mania, hypomania, and depression are absent.

−1   Slightly depressed, somewhat less energy than normal.

−2   Moderately slowed down, everything requires more effort than usual but can do daily activities.

−3   Very slowed down, feels overwhelmed by everything including small things, can do usual daily routine with much effort.

−4   Unable to do the usual major activities of daily life; worried, uptight, and despondent; judgment affected; thoughts distorted; suicidal thoughts; may be suicidal.

−5   Cannot do even the smallest activities of usual daily routine, barely able to get out of bed, no appetite, may have lost the will to live, likely to attempt suicide if not helped, should be hospitalized.

Figure 2.1.   Depression-Mania Ratings Scale.

cal examination to determine whether a physical illness other than bipolar disorder contributed to their symptoms. If you want to go into more depth for these and other individuals, more is to be found in the literature sold by the National Depressive and Manic-Depressive Association (Phone 312-642-0049; FAX 312-642-7243).

A higher rate of the disorder exists among wealthy persons. Some people with bipolar disorder are raised to be achievers and superachievers more so than those in the rest of the population. Perhaps these people tap into their "hyper" energy while exercising their creativity and talent, resulting in a rapid

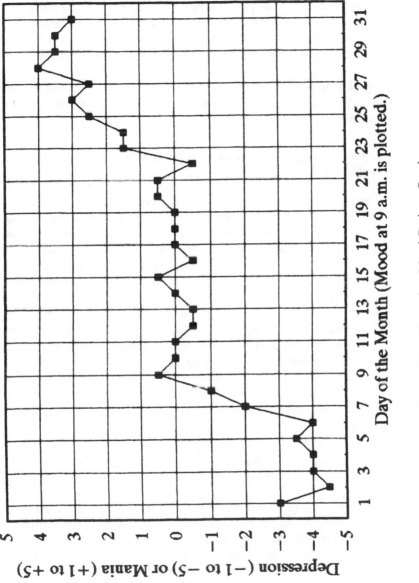

Figure 2.2. Example—Mood Ratings Graph.

"climbing of the ladder" to prosperity more often than those in the general population. Hypomania gives many people more drive and energy than normal, and they accomplish more than people who never experience hypomania. Perhaps their hypomania made them more extroverted and their abilities more noticeable to those who could promote them. The point here is that some with bipolar illness live a productive life and leave their valuable mark on the world.

Among all people, could creative individuals be the most sensitive to stimuli? Could their greater sensitivity make them more vulnerable to the stress necessary to initiate a mood disturbance?

Q-30. Aren't some drug and alcohol abusers really people with bipolar illness who are medicating their illness?

Yes. Some drug and alcohol abusers suffer from the symptoms of depression and mania, and they medicate themselves using "street" drugs and alcohol. Stimulants are used for depression, and depressants are used for mania. There are many forms of drugs used to medicate bipolar symptoms. For example, the legal drug alcohol can be used to "slow down" mania. These individuals may or may not know that they have an underlying bipolar illness; they only know that they have a problem. Diagnosing these individuals can be difficult because their illness is masked by drugs and alcohol. If there is a strong underlying illness such as bipolar disorder, the use of drugs and alcohol may have become addictive. After drugs and alcohol are removed from their system, the bipolar illness can be seen more easily, diagnosed accurately, and treated with the appropriate safe and legal medication. Most "street" drugs are potentially dangerous and carry lethal side effects in comparison with safe, monitored medications given by a physician; self-medication is not a satisfactory solution to bipolar symptoms.

Q-31. Are people with bipolar illness more violent than the general population?

Some people in the news media are guilty of stigmatizing and labeling all of us who have this disorder. Unfortunately for those of us with bipolar illness, newspeople add stigma by pointing out this illness among those who commit a violent crime. As a result, people falsely believe that all those with bipolar illness (called manic-depressives by the media) are equally prone to violence.

The truth is that about the same percentage of people with and without bipolar illness commit violent crimes. If a person has the moral tendency to harm others or commit violent crimes, the individual will commit them whether bipolar illness is present or not. People often become confused over which group of mentally ill people have the higher propensity for violence; it's people with paranoid schizophrenia, not people with bipolar disorder.

Q-32. While sleeping, is switching from depression or mania to a neutral mood (or vice versa) common for those with the disorder?

Many people with this illness claim that they felt fine when they went to sleep but awoke in the night (or towards morning) in the beginning of a mood disturbance.

One time I was severely depressed for a few weeks and actually felt close to dying. I went to sleep around 8 p.m. when I felt my worst, and I didn't expect to wake up again; however, at about 2 a.m. I woke up, and my depression had disappeared completely. During the following weeks, I remained in a neutral mood state. I'm not sure why I came out of depression in my sleep, but I do know that all my depressions ended "in the night."

At other times, I remember waking up in the middle of the night tossing and turning. My mind felt as if it were being charged or pressurized, and sleep was fragmented and difficult for the remainder of the night. The next day, I realized from my irritable mood that a hypomanic episode had begun.

Q-33. When I am manic or depressed, I have such vivid dreams. Is this common among those with my symptoms?

Yes. When I was not in a normal mood state, I dreamed fantastic dreams. Most of these dreams seemed very real, and they happened in 3-D color. I could feel, smell, and taste in my dreams. When I woke up, I didn't know where I was for about 10 seconds because the dream seemed like reality. Most of the dreams left an aftereffect for days that "colored" my mood and view of the world. The following are examples of dreams from my own life during my mood swings. When I was hypomanic, some of my dreams were futuristic, making the movie "Star Wars" seem like a small production. I have no idea from where the vivid content of these dreams came, because the images bore no resemblance to anything I had seen in the real world or in any movie. Perhaps they were "grand delusions" while sleeping or an imagination "gone wild." When I was depressed, my dreams were terrifying and made my heart pound. They usually contained the religious theme of me living at the end of the world and being viciously persecuted. Other horrible dreams placed me as a teenager living at home where "invisible monsters" were trying to kill me. Sometimes my home and family were being attacked by something angry and evil.

When I was either depressed or hypomanic, I had difficulty sleeping. I believe that I stayed in the dream stage of sleep much of the time because my sleep seemed shallow and short. In my normal mood state today, I seldom have these kinds of dreams with the frequency and intensity as I had before. Perhaps part of the explanation for the reduction of dreams is that I can sleep better and much deeper than before. The reason that I sleep better is because I'm taking medication, my stress level is down, and my moods are stable.

Q-34. I feel lousy and overwhelmed. Isn't the solution to ending my wide mood swings going to be just as giant and complex as my illness?

Absolutely not. My belief that the solution was very complicated, puzzling, and burdensome kept me from reaching out for help. I felt that the solution was going to take enormous effort on my part, and I didn't have any energy left to spare. I believed a doctor was going to have to sift through all the emotional wreckage of my life for answers, and I didn't want to go through that. Being overwhelmed, I talked myself out of seeking treatment.

I had a younger friend who had mood changes similar to mine. One time he was hospitalized for depression, and his doctor diagnosed him with bipolar disorder. My friend was given lithium and did much better. I was jealous and asked how he could get answers so fast while I had to wait and suffer with symptoms for years. My moods changed just as his had, and I thought that maybe I had bipolar disorder too. Being an engineer, I started to chart or graph my mood changes over three months. I clearly saw the cyclic nature of my mood changes, and I went to a psychologist with this in hand. The psychologist said that my mood changes had a biological origin, and he recommended a psychiatrist to me. Within a month, I started taking lithium. Several weeks later, all my depression and hypomania were gone, and they haven't returned in the last six years. I'm one of the 20% who take lithium and have almost no symptoms of the illness. I could not believe that the solution could be as simple as taking a pill. It was too good to be true. Yet it was true!

> Believe that answers to complex problems
> are a series of simple solutions.

Q-35. Do I need a physical examination prior to a diagnosis?

Yes. Initially you should have a thorough physical examination to evaluate your current medical condition; this would be used to rule out causes such as thyroid dysfunction, drug use, or other physical illness like multiple sclerosis.

Your body's organs will be evaluated to determine if they are functioning correctly and can tolerate the medications used to treat bipolar illness. For example, your heart would be evaluated to see if it has any problem that would be aggravated by the addition of medication. As part of the examination, a complete family history of all medical and mental conditions would be compiled to be used as an indication of what could be going wrong with your body and mind.

Q-36. What are my treatment alternatives for bipolar disorder?

If you have recurring manic episodes or major depressive episodes, taking medications is currently the most common way to relieve the majority of symptoms. No amount of psychotherapy sessions, support groups, diet changes, willpower, or exercises can compare even slightly with the effectiveness of the right medication. Most people with bipolar di⁚ ⁚ take medication as their major treatment. Some who are extremely d⁚ ⁚ manic may require electroconvulsive therapy (see Q-99) to⁚ ⁚ ⁚ir mood disturbance followed by long-term medication⁚

If you have hypoman⁚ ⁚sive symptoms and if you choose, you can function⁚ ⁚d disturbances. You may need to do some things to ma⁚ ⁚ns easier such as reducing stress, developing coping sk⁚ ⁚ the illness affects you specifically. You actually could ⁚ ⁚ or not to take medications.

Q-37. Is there a⁚

Research⁚ ⁚treatment of bipolar disorder is always ongoing, but a⁚ ⁚ has not yet been found. Medications usually relieve ma⁚ ⁚s of the illness, and some people have no more sympto⁚ ⁚ter going on medication. Many live an acceptable life with⁚ ⁚mptoms; however, a relative few spend a lifetime sifting⁚ ⁚s while still experiencing significant symptoms. No guarantee e⁚ ⁚dividual living with bipolar disorder can be completely relieve⁚ ⁚ptoms.

Q-38. What does the future hold for us in understanding and treating bipolar disorder?

Here are some areas where medical research continues, and where future benefits for people with bipolar disorder lie.

1. Identification of the exact gene(s) causing the illness and the biochemical reactions that are controlled by these genes.
2. More effective medications with fewer side effects.
3. Understanding brain function (including the mind) as it relates to bipolar illness.
4. Understanding environmental contributions to the illness.
5. Better ability to predict who will inherit bipolar disorder.

If the advances in treatment of bipolar illness of the last 15 years are an indication of the next 15 years, our future is bright, and there will be much progress.

PR-2A. A PSYCHIATRIST'S ADDITION

Bipolar disorders are divided into three different subtypes. The first one is Bipolar-I, which is a bipolar depression with mania. Mania is characterized by a mood that is either elevated, expansive, or irritable, and the disturbance is sufficiently severe as to cause marked impairment or to require hospitalization. Some patients are psychotic with delusions, paranoia, and bizarre behavior. Manic patients tend to exhibit grandiosity, a decreased need for sleep, distractibility, excessive focus on goal-directed activity, agitation, and excessive involvement in pleasurable activities that may get the patient in trouble. Spending large sums of money for trivial or nonessential items, sexual adventures, excessive drinking, and speeding on the highway represent activities unrecognized by the individual as dangerous or potentially dangerous. This person also would have a history of major depressive episodes.

Bipolar-II disorder includes major depressive episodes and cycles of hypomania. Hypomania is identical to mania, but the symptoms are not severe enough to cause significant impairment in usual activities or to require hospitalization. Delusions are never present, and all other symptoms tend to be less severe than in manic episodes. The diagnostic requirements for all bipolar disorders are given in the DSM-IV.

Cyclothymia is a third category of bipolar disorder where symptoms of hypomania and depression occur and recur with natural remissions and seasonal patterns with alternating moods lasting for months at a time leaving periods of normality in most. Some individuals alternate between being very enthusiastic, optimistic, up, and describing themselves as in a happy mood with more than normal "down" periods where the individual would describe himself or herself as depressed, despondent, and unable to enjoy life. These moods do not affect the individual's functioning significantly but obviously cause problems not only for himself, but also for family, friends, and work relationships.

I would diagnosis Bryan as having Bipolar-II Disorder. He has never been hospitalized and, although he has been impaired and has had difficulty functioning, he never has had a manic episode where he has been so dysfunctional that he has been unable to work or function socially. When those in our society think of bipolar illness, they fail to recognize that many are similar to Bryan.

Bipolar illness is a relatively common psychiatric disorder and, upon careful questioning, one nearly always can discover a familial history with parents, grandparents, or first order relatives also suffering from a bipolar disorder. A significant change has occurred in the medical and mental health communities in that today the diagnosis of Bryan's bipolar disorder would have been made immediately rather than many years after he first sought assistance. This disorder is now recognized and regularly diagnosed and treated, often by the family physician or the primary care physician; however, because psychiatrists have the time, experience, and extensive training in the treatment of this disorder, they are the physician of choice rather than any other medical doctor.

PR-2B. A PSYCHIATRIST'S RESPONSE

This is a superb chapter that goes into great detail to help you understand how to differentiate words such as mania and hypomania and how to tell if you are just hyper or whether you are hypomanic. It clearly outlines the only symptoms for this diagnosis that a doctor can use to make a diagnosis of bipolar disorder.

No laboratory tests, no x-ray, and no physical examination are known that would help the doctor make a diagnosis. What enables the doctor to make the diagnosis of bipolar disorder is the patient's history as well as the symptoms exhibited by the patient in the doctor's office.

You will notice that Bryan did not show any signs or symptoms of hypomania while in the doctor's office, thus causing his first doctor to miss the diagnosis of bipolar and to treat him primarily as having a depression. The psychotherapy following a misdiagnosis is a long, difficult, arduous, expensive, and mostly ineffective process. If the doctor diagnoses the patient as having a major depression and not as a bipolar disorder, the treatment and approach to the disorder will be significantly different from that which one would take if a diagnosis of bipolar were made.

In this first section, questions that the patient, family, and friends have about the illness are explored thoroughly.

RELATIONSHIP
WITH THE DOCTOR

Every person with bipolar disorder with whom I have talked has had both good and bad experiences with psychiatrists. The doctor who failed to give a correct diagnosis is resented by the patient who had to suffer greatly with symptoms for quite awhile. The doctor who has treated bipolar disorder adequately is held in high regard and is valued like gold by the patient. This section is an attempt to bridge the gap between doctors and their mental health clients by answering common questions from people at a bipolar support group. The answers are meant to be enlightening for both doctors and patients, and the responses that follow are not meant to put down or degrade psychiatric professionals. Finally, these questions provide mental health consumers with the knowledge they need to get more for their limited finances.

**Q-39. I might have a bipolar disorder. Should I seek treatment
from a psychiatrist or a psychologist?**

A psychiatrist is a medical doctor (M.D.) who specializes in psychiatry. A psychologist is a person who has a doctorate (Ph.D.) in psychology but is not a medical doctor. Because bipolar disorder is a biological illness and its treatment medical in nature, a psychiatrist is the one you should see. Also, only a psychiatrist can prescribe and monitor medications effectively. Your family doctor, internist, or G.P. (general practitioner) is able to prescribe medications, but he or she usually won't have the detailed knowledge about the illness necessary for adequate treatment.

29

Q-40. Are doctors people too?

Yes. Doctors feel the same emotions that we do. At some time in their careers, almost all psychiatrists have felt afraid that a patient may commit suicide and most have experienced grief when a patient did commit suicide. Others may have felt anger or even some hatred for a patient. As a result, they may have said something they regretted later. Most doctors probably have had a patient flirt with them, but in general probably only a small minority of doctors have flirted with patients. Psychiatrists can manage all of these situations because they put their other patients and their own feelings aside and help *you* solve *your* problems. Furthermore, they are trained not to let their emotions interfere in your treatment. If doctors got emotionally involved with all their patients, they soon would be overwhelmed and have to stop practicing psychiatry for lack of energy.

I'm sure you will discover that there are not two types of humans, psychiatrists and ordinary people. Doctors are just like everyone else except that they have some unique talents with medicine and in working with people, and they must have great patience and endurance to listen to patients eight hours or more a day. They are intelligent and work hard. They are experts at managing their time and energy, and we can learn a great deal by their example. Most are psychiatrists because they enjoy practicing medicine, and because they love people. They are not perfect and make mistakes. All the psychiatrists whom I have known have families, and their families require the same amount of time, devotion, and nurturing as other families. What we, as patients and outsiders, don't see are their personally decorated houses, varied hobbies, family relationships, and other activities. We don't see that the doctor has a life outside the office. Perhaps that is why you asked the question—are doctors people too?

Q-41. What are the qualities of a good psychiatrist?

The following are some of the admirable qualities that I have found in previous doctors, and these reflect the opinions of my support group members too. A good psychiatrist

1. knows the latest about bipolar disorder.
2. is highly knowledgeable about treatment including the medication that I'm taking and its side effects.
3. knows when to refer me to a specialist, if needed.
4. doesn't "throw" prescription drugs at me or become a "pill pusher."

5. takes the time to get an accurate diagnosis.
6. listens to what I say.
7. shows genuine concern for me.
8. treats me as an important person, not just another patient or client.
9. does not take advantage of my weaknesses for personal gain or enjoyment.
10. tells me what I need to hear in a sensitive way.
11. doesn't have to be reminded to do routine medical tests required for people taking certain medications.
12. engages in a dialogue with me as opposed to someone who seldom speaks and just takes notes.
13. doesn't talk all the time but won't allow me to do all the talking.
14. doesn't engage in lengthy, regular conversations regarding subjects irrelevant to my treatment such as hobbies or other out-of-the-office interests.
15. begins my session on time and ends it on time—is time conscious.
16. is accessible.

Q-42. How do I find a good psychiatrist?

We all want to find a doctor who can give us a completely accurate diagnosis with the least expensive treatment. In the psychiatric profession, as in all professions, a few doctors graduate at the top of the their class and others at the bottom. The vast majority are in the middle. Also, psychiatrists may specialize in different areas, and some may have an area that they consider to be their subject of expertise. So we, as consumers, have to "hunt" for the best doctor, and suggested starting places follow.

1. Many members of a bipolar disorder support group are more than willing to refer you to a doctor. Ask for opinions from the group and from the group facilitator. See Q-139 for the location of support groups.
2. National Depressive and Manic-Depressive Association. See Q-139 for the address and phone number.
3. National Alliance for the Mentally Ill. See Q-139 for the address and phone number.
4. Your county mental health association may know of a psychiatrist locator service. The list may not reflect the full list of psychiatrists, and it won't reflect which doctor is the best.
5. Look in the yellow pages of your telephone book under Physicians, Psychiatry.
6. Your family doctor can recommend someone.

Q-43. I have bipolar disorder, and I am a member of my employer's Health Maintenance Organization (HMO) with a limited pool of psychiatrists. How do I find a good psychiatrist?

With a small number of psychiatrists in an HMO, the pool of knowledge concerning specific areas of psychiatry could be limited. Obviously, your options are limited, but there are a few things you can do to help your situation. Discuss your problem at a bipolar support group and see if someone else is a member of your HMO; you then could get his or her recommendation for a good doctor. Ask your HMO for a list of its psychiatrists, and ask if you can choose from among their staff of doctors; then call and interview doctors as described in Q-45. Send a letter to your HMO and request that they provide the doctor you have picked; tell them why this doctor is best for you. You might have to be assertive with them eventually, but start with a neutral tone. If you have tried all of these paths and are not getting satisfactory health care, complain directly to your employer's benefits department. As a customer of an HMO, you have the right to receive the adequate treatment for which you have paid in premiums. Get your company fighting for you, and don't stop until you have what you want. In the end, you'll probably receive the doctor of your choice within the HMO, or the HMO may allow you to see a more specialized psychiatrist who isn't part of their group at no increase in expense to you.

Q-44. Should I choose a man or a woman for a psychiatrist?

Obviously, both male and female doctors are capable of giving excellent treatment for a bipolar disorder. Being a man or a woman doesn't have any effect on whether someone can diagnose your illness correctly and prescribe suitable medication(s). If you need psychotherapy, having a male or female doctor *can* influence the outcome. For example, if you are a man and grew up with difficulties bonding to the same sex, you might want to choose a male doctor who could help you work through those feelings. The choice is yours.

Q-45. Isn't one psychiatrist as good as another?

No! Some doctors have more knowledge about this illness than others. And among those doctors, as in all professions, some are more competent than others. A common complaint among people with bipolar illness is that they have spent time and money on a doctor for treatment that was not helpful. So making a wise choice in doctors at the beginning is the key to getting on the road to recovery now. Once you have several names of doctors as a result of Q-42, follow these additional steps to ensure that you have a good doctor.

1. Talk briefly to psychiatrists over the phone to see if they are compatible enough with you to go in for a visit. If they can't spend five minutes on the phone with you in a period of a week, they aren't for you.
2. As part of the first visit, interview your doctor. Have your questions prepared ahead of time.
3. Ask for the doctor's references and get a prospective doctor's resume.
4. If you still have any doubts about a doctor, call your state medical board (listed in the phone book in the government pages, under State Government Offices, Medical Board of "Your State," Verification of Licenses), and get their input as to whether a doctor under consideration is completely ethical and competent. Ask whether the doctor has been involved in any legal trouble such as malpractice. Ask what the doctor's professional record looks like?

Something to think about . . . I'll bet most of us spend more time looking for a good auto mechanic than searching for a good psychiatrist. Which is more important?

Q-46. Is spiritual or religious compatibility between my psychiatrist and myself desirable?

If you both have the same belief system and values, you have a common denominator or basis for resolving conflicts and making decisions over the issues that come up in psychotherapy. You may find it easier to accept the advice of your doctor, and you may feel much more comfortable sharing your life's details with a "kindred spirit." If this issue is important to you, find out what your doctor's spiritual or religious beliefs are during your *first* visit.

Q-47. What should I do to be a good patient?

The following list contains your responsibilities in the doctor-patient relationship, and these are essential for maintaining a good relationship with your doctor.

1. Be on time to appointments.
2. Pay bills on time.
3. Let your doctor know of cancellations well ahead of time (A 24-hour notice is common).
4. Do your part to fill out insurance forms, and file them on time.
5. Come to an appointment with a short list of the most pressing topics for discussion.

6. Let your doctor know about new symptoms or side effects when they appear.
7. Give your doctor the chance to have input in all relevant areas of your life.
8. Always be open and honest.
9. Let the doctor give the diagnosis and prognosis.
10. Cooperate with your doctor, and follow through with whatever you and your doctor decide.
11. If treatment is good for you, stick with it even though it might be painful or distressing.
12. If you don't like something that your doctor is doing, discuss it right away.
13. Treat your doctor the way that you want to be treated.
14. Keep your mind turned on, and ask questions.
15. Be a partner with your doctor in your treatment, and don't fall into the passive role of the doctor-fix-me syndrome.
16. Don't change your medication or dosage without consulting with your doctor.

Q-48. Will psychotherapy help me?

There are many types of psychotherapy, but all of them essentially are trying to treat a mental or emotional disorder by psychological means. The purpose of psychotherapy is to experience and process past painful feelings and memories repeatedly so that you eventually can recall the painful memories without feeling. Psychotherapy is good at processing and resolving buried emotions from earlier traumatic experiences, and it will remove the heavy weight of "emotional baggage" from yesterday's events so that you can get on with living in the present.

Psychotherapy would be valuable if you have depression caused by the loss of your job or a death in the family, but psychotherapy will not end depression caused by a biochemical process from your bipolar disorder. However, psychotherapy is valuable for dealing with your feelings about your illness, repairing damaged relationships caused in part by the illness, and helping you with related living problems.

Q-49. I have some "deep dark secrets." Do I need to tell them to my doctor?

Yes. For the four psychiatrists whom I have seen, every one of them has been compassionate and supportive when I "let it all out." At first, I was embarrassed and afraid to tell someone else exactly who I was and what I had done, but I discovered that my doctor had "heard it all before." Doctors are paid to help me and not put me down. They are trained to be nonjudgmental, objective, and uncritical. I had to give my doctors all the "pieces of the puzzle" that composed my life before they could put them together correctly and give me a completely accurate diagnosis.

You should open up and divulge the total contents and burdens within because some of them may have a direct impact on your moods. If you have problems such as drug abuse, alcoholism, sexual abuse, unresolved sexuality issues, relationship difficulties, job difficulties, legal trouble, and family secrets, these can affect your mood greatly. You may be discouraged or stressed by these secrets, and these symptoms may provide a triggering mechanism for depression and possibly mania. Your doctor needs the whole picture in view, and let the doctor decide which issues need to be dealt with first. Bringing up other health problems and potentially embarrassing family medical history may bring more light into the overall scene. Sometimes when people are manic or depressed, they do things that are illegal, immoral, or obscene, and these need to be brought out into the open and discussed if they apply to you. Then your doctor will be more able to identify your behavior and characteristics and help you lower your arousal state over them. If you only give your doctor part of the story, you might end up with an inadequate partial treatment.

> Garbage in, garbage out.
> The whole story in, accurate diagnosis out.
> What's the wise choice?

Q-50. Will my problem with authority figures affect my relationship with my doctor?

If you grew up with a certain authority figure, such as a parent who abused his or her power or authority over you in some way, this experience may show itself in the dynamics between you and your doctor. For example, the minute your doctor plays an authoritative role or tells you what to do, you may get a rise in resentment or anger. These feelings would only be a replay of "old tapes" written internally by you about an abusive authority figure while you were a child. It wouldn't be a real expression of anger towards the doctor, but it's a remembrance of anger towards your parent(s) or other authority figure(s). Obviously, your doctor is not your mother or father, and your doctor is not in authority over you. If you experience these emotions while in psychotherapy, work through the feelings with your doctor. Processing your anger with your psychiatrist will lead to better emotional health. Don't be afraid of your anger or resentment. Be open and express yourself; let it out.

Q-51. I have just been diagnosed with bipolar disorder, and I am seeing a psychiatrist twice a week. Do I have to go to a psychiatrist that frequently in the future?

It depends. After you become stabilized on medications, you can reduce your visits to maintenance visits. These shorter visits may be needed monthly or every six weeks, for example, and last 20 or 30 minutes each. The doctor may draw blood for a lithium level and talk to you briefly about what's happening in your life. Also, these shorter visits may cost slightly more than one half of the regular session rate.

On the other hand, unresolved issues may be present in your life and may cause mood disruptions for which you may need or want psychotherapy. In that case, your doctor might recommend more visits until your situation is resolved.

Q-52. Will some psychiatrists reduce their hourly rate for me because I just cannot afford it?

It depends on the doctor. If a psychiatrist has a time slot open for a new patient and has three full-paying people trying to get in, why would the doctor want to give a rate break to anyone? Fortunately, only a minority of doctors are this money-centered, and most are sensitive to the needs of people who aren't wealthy and don't have fabulous insurance policies. They budget a few reduced rate openings into their schedule, and if these aren't filled up, you could fit in. Although the doctor might be affordable, don't forget to ask yourself whether or not the doctor is the one who really can help you.

Q-53. When I give my doctor money for a 50-minute session, I feel that I'm paying for friendship. I don't like that, and I'm confused. Is something wrong with my thinking?

First, look at these seven components of a friendship and ask yourself whether or not they are present in your doctor-patient relationship.

1. Are you and your doctor *mutually* drawn to each other as with your other friendships?
2. Are you and your doctor each other's companion and ally?

3. Does your doctor love you the way your other friends do?
4. Do you and your doctor share common spiritual beliefs or values?
5. Do you and your doctor go out to eat, go the movies, go exercise, or watch TV together as you do with your other friends?
6. Do you have similar interests and hobbies?
7. Do you have a two-way sharing of intimate secrets?

The answer to most of these questions is probably no. Although your doctor may be quite friendly, you should think of your doctor as a service provider rather than as a typical friend; your doctor is providing treatment, and you pay for it. Some patients feel reluctant to change doctors because they feel that they are rejecting a "friend." The process of changing doctors will be much easier if you have a service provider mentality than if you have a strong one-way friendship bond to your doctor.

I have a couple of other points to make. Very rarely you may become friends, in the complete sense of the word, with your doctor and relate outside of the office. If this happens, don't hesitate to change doctors if the need arises. Finally, all the doctors whom I know have been friendly in a professional way, and they surely haven't been enemies!

Q-54. My doctor doesn't return my calls in a reasonable length of time. What should I do?

Most doctors stay very busy and have a full schedule, but they have breaks of 10 to 15 minutes between sessions with patients. This short amount of time can be reduced further by sessions that run over. Sometimes the doctor may be doing lab work on someone in the office during the break between sessions, and occasionally your doctor may leave to visit a patient at a hospital. At other times, your doctor may have to return urgent calls from other patients or interact with drug sales people or even legal professionals. Normally, you can reach your doctor if you call during the break period, but time your call right to the minute. If you reach a receptionist, nurse, or someone else, leave a brief message and ask that your doctor call you back between patients' sessions as soon as possible; have the message marked urgent if appropriate. Since your doctor usually has only a few minutes to talk, be to the point and don't expect to discuss any issues at length.

You are paying your doctor for a service that includes him or her being reasonably accessible, and most doctors encourage their patients to call if they have a problem or a short question. If your doctor has a history of not calling you back within a few hours, and you can't get your doctor to call by leaving messages or calling "on the hour," express your legitimate complaint to your doctor.

Q-55. If I think I'm in an emergency situation in the middle of the night, should I call my doctor?

Yes. I suggest that you discuss this question with your doctor in the first session and prior to taking any medication. Here are some other related things to do.

1. Ask your doctor to define the circumstances that would require you to make an emergency call.
2. Find out what your doctor's attitude is towards calls in the middle of the night.
3. Get your doctor's emergency *and* home phone numbers, if available.
4. If your doctor's phone is transferred to an answering service, find out how long it usually takes for your doctor to return calls.
5. If you are unable to reach your doctor, find out who you should call.

When you need help, don't hesitate to call!

Q-56. I know that I have been accurately diagnosed with a bipolar disorder, but I seem to have reached a point where I don't feel my doctor is doing me any more good. Should I change doctors?

One big reason why patients want to change doctors is that their symptoms of the illness are still present. After spending a reasonable length of time (e.g., four to six months) trying to eliminate or reduce your manic and depressive periods through medication, you still could have partial symptoms of the illness; this is not uncommon. One reason for this could be that finding suitable medications for you is difficult, and a lengthy trial-and-error approach is required. Or perhaps you are one of the unfortunate few who cannot find a good solution for your symptoms with medication, but keep looking and don't give up. Another reason could be that your doctor isn't using the latest treatment approaches or pharmacology properly, and I know from personal experience that this happens. If you believe that you have run into a dead end because you can't eliminate symptoms of your illness through your doctor, seeking treatment from a new doctor should be seriously considered.

The second reason why patients want to change doctors deals with the use of psychotherapy. When some patients get close to a breakthrough in solving a psychological or emotional issue, they want to bolt out of the doctor's office rather than experience the emotions uncovered in therapy. Subconsciously, this desire to not experience feelings related to an issue may come out as wanting to change doctors. This may not apply to you, but give it good honest consideration. Furthermore, you may discover that your doctor doesn't have sufficient knowledge and experience to help you in the specific area where you need psychotherapy, and this may be the reason for feeling that you have done all that is possible with your doctor.

Discuss the above two areas with your doctor. After you have given yourself some time to think this over, you'll know whether or not to find another doctor.

Q-57. How do I tell my psychiatrist that I will not be coming back because I have decided to change doctors?

I assume that you have decided on a different doctor because you are not getting significant help from your current doctor. Almost all patients change doctors at some time, and each relationship may have its uncomfortable moments associated with its end. Telling your doctor face to face about your decision to move on is the best form of communication. Although it is as simple as speaking the words, ending your doctor-patient relationship can cause some anxiety. If you feel intimidated, write your doctor a letter, and have your doctor call you to discuss your decision if necessary. If you haven't discussed with your doctor your reason for leaving, I suggest that you give an explanation to your doctor to add closure to the relationship. You should consider making your "exit" in a thoughtful, mature manner because you might need your previous doctor's assistance for some endeavor in the future.

As an example of terminating a relationship with a doctor, think of the service your dentist provides. Would the dentist's feelings be hurt if you left for another dentist? The answer is no because the dentist is a service provider rather than your buddy. We should feel the same way towards our psychiatrist; think of it as changing a service rather than as ending a friendship. Your doctor understands that it is a professional relationship that you are ending. You don't even need to give your doctor a two-week notice.

If you are taking medication, having another doctor lined up is very important. Don't let weeks or months pass by without having a doctor monitor your medical condition.

Put your mental health first in all your decisions!

PR-3. A PSYCHIATRIST'S RESPONSE

Yes, "doctors are people too," and doctors do feel the same emotions as their patients. One of the most basic components of a successful therapeutic relationship is the ability of the doctor to feel the feelings that the patient has. That means that the doctor has empathy, or the ability to empathize with his or her patients; however, this poses a serious problem.

Patients with a bipolar disorder have very intense feelings of depression, as well as intense feelings of elation, excitement, irritation, or the other symptoms of mania or hypomania. The patient comes to the doctor in pain, and pain is a feeling one does not want to have. The patient comes to the doctor to gain relief from the emotional or psychological pain. Neither the doctor, nor the patient, want to feel or experience painful feelings while in the doctor's office. These feelings are not only uncomfortable for the patient, but they are uncomfortable for the empathic physician; however, if the doctor is unable or unwilling to feel with the patient, then the therapy is useless. Certainly, the doctor can be wise and teach the patient how to cope with a bipolar disordered life; but this is not psychotherapy, and the patient is not getting his or her money's worth. One can read a book or attend free educational support groups to learn how to cope with the illness.

One of the most important tools used to deal with past painful feeling memories that interfere significantly with the patient's life is psychotherapy. The patient and the doctor must have a contract, or an agreement, that the patient will pay the doctor to listen, identify, interpret, and *feel* the painful feelings that he or she is experiencing.

What good is that? If the patient is able to engage and express his or her feelings to the physician repeatedly, and the physician truly listens, hears, and "walks" with the patient as the circumstances of the painful feelings are engaged, the feelings will be reduced over time. For example, surely one of the most painful experiences one can have is the loss of a loved one. That individual must grieve or feel the pain, the sadness, and the loneliness of the loss. The doctor must feel that same pain, the same feelings of sadness, loneliness, and hopelessness, so that the patient eventually becomes less pained by that experience of loss. Ultimately, the patient will be able to engage that memory and it will no longer be painful. This is successful treatment. This is psychotherapy.

MEDICATIONS IN GENERAL

Q-58. Do all people with bipolar illness have to be hospitalized to go on medications?

No. If someone is suicidal, has extreme mania, or is psychotic, however, then hospitalization may be necessary for the person to go on medications. Close monitoring of reactions to medications and medications' effectiveness during the first few weeks is very important, and this is difficult for suicidal, manic, or psychotic people without hospitalization. The side effects of medication could overload and disorient a suicidal person, and that person may attempt suicide. In extreme mania, a person could feel "great" and may not see the need for the drugs or not take them as directed. A psychotic person could be living in another reality where drugs are viewed as not beneficial or even as a threat to their reality. All these individuals need close, constant supervision and care in a hospital setting if they are going to get better, and to be hospitalized is usually a decision made by a psychiatrist based on the person's needs.

When I started taking lithium, I wasn't hospitalized. I had a job and continued to work a 28-hour week without interruption from the addition of lithium. I have never been hospitalized for going on medications, and I know many with bipolar illness who have had similar experiences. However, if I have to make quick significant changes in medications in the future, I'll probably want to be hospitalized because the side effects from withdrawal can cause great anxiety, disorientation, and instability in my life.

For any situation in my life that includes going on medications, I have my doctor give me guidance and encouragement and my support friends give their experience and understanding.

Q-59. Will I stop feeling emotions when I go on medications?

No. The mood stabilizing drugs, antidepressants, and antipsychotics will not prevent you from feeling the normal range of emotions. You will still experience joy and sadness, but they will be in response to something happening in the world around you or because you choose them. You probably have felt a wide range of moods with your bipolar illness, but these were not associated with anything going on in "the real world." The illness caused these unpredictable ups and downs, not your external environment or your reaction to it. After going on medications, your true emotions still will be intact, but the mood disturbances caused by your illness hopefully will be gone.

Q-60. I have a fear of going on these "powerful medications." How can I be more at ease with them?

The best way to overcome your fear is to gain knowledge about your illness and what these psychotropic drugs can do for you. (*Psychotropic* means "acting on the mind.") Fear of the unknown comes into play for all those with bipolar illness at the start of medications to some degree or another. If you are able, completely research the drugs that you will take or have begun to take, and find out their effectiveness and potential for side effects. For a range of experiences, ask members of a bipolar support group for their experience with your medications, and ask your doctor about expectations for your medications. Everything you do to increase your knowledge about what is happening will diminish your fear and strengthen your confidence. Take it one day at a time.

Q-61. Are these medications addictive?

I haven't heard of anyone getting addicted to a mood stabilizer, an antidepressant, or an antipsychotic drug; these aren't addictive drugs. If you have doubts about the addictive potential of your specific medication, ask your doctor and/or pharmacist about it.

For many of these psychotropic drugs, side effects associated with withdrawal are very possible, and these sensations often are mistaken for signs of addiction; however, side effects are not the same as addiction. Going off a drug can take several days or a week or two, and the changes that your mind has to go through during that process can cause a wide range of discomfort. After the medication is out of your body, you won't have any craving, desire, or obsession to be back on the medication as you would if you were addicted.

Q-62. What are some of the side effects from medications used to treat bipolar disorder?

Although knowledge of the possible side effects of medications can instill fear in people, this information can be used to combat fears associated with psychotropic drugs. Side effects from medications can be categorized into the corresponding 12 areas of the body listed below. This is only a partial list and does not include a thorough compilation of all the side effects from medications used to treat the symptoms of bipolar illness. Most of these side effects are very rare. When beginning a new medication, you will probably experience only a few side effects changing every few days to some other side effects. I have italicized the effects that I have experienced, and most of them were temporary. After reading this list, I'm sure you will agree that we need a doctor to monitor our health.

1. Central Nervous System (your brain and body's nerves). (sedation, *drowsiness,* lethargy, fatigue, *muscle weakness,* emotional upset, *tremor,* headache, confusion, restlessness, *dizziness,* vertigo, stupor, blackouts, impaired speech, incoordination, hyperexcitability, hallucinations, psychosis, aggression, hyperactivity, behavioral deterioration, insomnia, and nervousness)
2. Cardiovascular (heart and blood vessels). (ankle and wrist swelling, low blood pressure, high blood pressure, slowed heartbeat, reversible electrocardiogram changes, aggravation of coronary artery disease, and inflammation of a vein with or without blood clot formation)
3. Skin (outer). (itching, rash, urticaria, and abnormal redness of the skin)
4. Eye, ear, nose and throat. (inflammatory diseases of the mouth, salivating too much, ringing in the ears, conjunctivitis, *dry mouth* and pharynx, blurred vision, double vision, aggravation of narrow-angle glaucoma, pigmentation in the eyes, and involuntary eye movements)
5. Gastrointestinal (mouth, esophagus, stomach, intestines). (*nausea,* vomiting, indigestion, anorexia, *diarrhea, thirst, metallic taste,* taste change, abdominal pain or cramps, inflammation of the tongue, *increased appetite and weight gain,* and pancreatitis)
6. Genitourinary (genital and urinary organs or functions). (excessive amount of urine, abnormal amounts of sugar in the urine, incontinence, de-

creased renal [kidney] concentrating capacity, urinary frequency or retention, impotence, the presence of albumin in the urine, elevated blood urea nitrogen levels, and urinary tract infection)
7. Hematologic (blood and blood-forming organs). (white blood cell abnormality such as eosinophilia, an increase in white blood cells, and inhibited platelet aggregation)
8. Hepatic (liver). (enzyme level elevations, abnormal liver function tests, and hepatitis)
9. Metabolic. (elevated serum ammonia levels, transient hyperglycemia, goiter, hypothyroidism, and calcium deficiency)
10. Respiratory. (flu-like syndrome, upper respiratory infection, pharyngitis, cough, and bronchitis)
11. Local. (irritation around injection sites)
12. Other. (hair loss, curling or waving of hair, profuse perspiration, fever, chills, pulmonary sensitivity, paralysis, photosensitivity, abnormal movements, leg cramps, and joint pain)

When beginning medications, I was driving down a two-lane road with a friend, and there in front was a car stopped in my lane. I had no thought of stopping, because my mind was distracted; I was daydreaming. Then my friend said just in time, "Aren't you going to stop?" Had my friend not been with me, I would have wrecked my car and injured myself, my friend, and perhaps others. Watch out for those sneaky side effects while driving!

Q-63. How do I know when a medication is wrong for me?

If a medication has dangerous side effects or too many undesirable side effects, the medication is wrong for you. The following are some of the possible life-threatening side effects for medications used to treat bipolar disorder. It should be noted that these effects are *very rare* and, if they were present to a significant degree among those taking a specific medication, the drug wouldn't be on the market. The effects are as follows:

agranulocytosis (severe decrease in blood granulocytes),
aplastic anemia (defective functioning of blood-forming bone marrow),
arrhythmias,
peripheral circulatory collapse,
coma,
congestive heart failure,
toxic hepatitis,
nephrotoxicity (poisoning of the kidneys),
seizures,

thrombocytopenia (persistent decrease in the number of blood platelets), and
increased bleeding time.

Q-64. Should I be concerned about interactions with other drugs?

Before you start any new medication, you should consult with your doctor *and* your pharmacist over whether the new medication(s) will cause any adverse reactions with your current medications. This applies to both over-the-counter medications and prescription drugs. Your doctor may not know all the adverse reactions, but your pharmacist's computer (assuming there is a computer) should have the latest. In general, pharmacists are more than willing to answer your questions, and they will do it for free. Other secondary methods for evaluating new medications include reading the product information sheet (your pharmacist usually has this), calling the drug manufacturer, and looking it up in a drug handbook.

As a rule, when in any doubt, check it out.

Q-65. I want the freedom to continue to drink alcohol or use drugs such as marijuana, cocaine, LSD, etc. as I did before going on meds. Will there be any interactions with my medications?

Because people's bodies and their medications differ widely, evaluating and predicting exactly what your response to alcohol and marijuana would be is difficult. You should discuss this with your doctor and follow your doctor's recommendation. For drugs other than alcohol and marijuana, more serious interactions with your medications probably will result; coma and even death could occur. As a rule, if you aren't 100% sure of the outcome of drug use, don't do it. As another rule, don't use any drugs just because somebody you know did it and didn't get hurt.

I have some concerns and questions about the possibility of your use of "street" drugs. Why would you want to use one or more mood altering substances after spending considerable time and money to stabilize your moods? Won't you be complicating the efforts to identify what your *normal* mood state is? How will your doctor decide whether the side effects you feel are due to your medication or your "street" drugs? How will you determine whether or not your medication is effective? Do you realize that trouble with the law over these drugs could wreck your mental health and your future? Knowing that not all "street" drugs are the same, what would happen if the drug content of what

you would consume wasn't what you thought it was? Do you have a drug problem and need help with it? Wouldn't you be playing dangerous games with
your mental health? Whatever you do, it's your choice, and *choices have consequences.*

If you drink alcohol or use "street" drugs,
tell your doctor right away!

Q-66. What is the best way to listen accurately to my body's response to medications?

Get rid of anything going into your body that could affect your mood and
energy level. These include caffeine from coffee, tea, soft drinks, chocolate,
and some over-the-counter pain medications. Because some people have reactions to food additives such as MSG, or Nutrasweet, these should be considered
for removal. Of course, alcohol, or any "street" drug would hinder your ability
to listen to your body's response too. A more difficult substance to eliminate is
nicotine.

With your body back as close to normal as possible, you could assess accurately the side effects and overall effectiveness of the medications you have
begun to take or have been taking. Also, you'll be better able to recognize the
beginning "edge" of a mood disturbance sooner than if you were consuming
substances that would affect your mood and energy level.

Knowing your body's base line is important. You'll know if that sluggishness in the morning is an everyday occurrence caused by lingering depression
or too little sleep. You'll know whether that drowsiness in the afternoon comes
from caffeine withdrawal, your medication, or depression. If you are "hyper"
and haven't had any caffeine, you'll know that you're getting hypomanic or
manic. You'll know if your medication causes heavy drowsiness before bedtime when all your stimulants have been removed. Without caffeine, you will
know that your tossing and turning at night was due to something other than
too much caffeine, perhaps the beginning of a mood disturbance.

Q-67. Where can I find prescription drugs at the best price?

I suggest that you shop and compare prices in different drug stores for
both name brands and generic brands. A generic brand is cheaper than a name
brand, but not all prescription drugs come in generic. Calling large stores will
help you find the best price, and the savings could be significant. Ask your

doctor and your support group for their recommendation for a pharmacy. Also, there are some mail order pharmacies that could have lower costs.

For several years, doctors gave me prescriptions for 25mg and 50mg of an antidepressant because my usual dosage was 75mg per day. One day when I went to refill my prescriptions, a pharmacist gave me the manufacturer's product information sheet for the antidepressant. To my surprise, the manufacturer made a whole range of dosage sizes including a 75mg capsule. One prescription for 75mg capsules was a whole lot cheaper than the previous two prescriptions combined. Knowing what dosages are manufactured may save you money on your prescriptions.

Q-68. During the first few weeks after I started my medications, I was irritable. Is this normal?

For many, yes. Irritability or extreme sensitivity towards others and the environment is common when going on or off of some medications used to treat a bipolar disorder. For some individuals, the irritability manifests itself with the urge to "snap someone's head off." For others, it may be a spontaneous decision to end a relationship that has some problems. Overreacting to minor and trivial events is probably the most common sign of this irritability.

I lost some good friends because of my angry outbursts and behavior while starting lithium, and a few other relationships took months to put back together. You would be wise to warn all the people you care about that you may not be yourself for a while due to medication changes. If you start to get irritable, you can recognize it for what it is and keep your actions or reactions from developing into a rage or angry outburst.

Q-69. I recently started taking medication for my bipolar illness, and I feel the urge to quit my job and "get away from it all." Do you think this change is a good idea?

Many who have been in your same situation have had the urge to escape to safeguard that last remaining piece of creativity or sensitivity within that they think has been untouched by the illness or unaltered by medications. Making big decisions concerning relationships, jobs, and finances is not wise during the transition period. If it is an important decision, can't it wait until you have become stabilized on medications? Won't you make better decisions when you aren't depressed or manic? During this "escape," will you really have all the support from family, friends, and support groups that you need? Will your doctor be able to monitor your progress in the way that is necessary and safe?

When you start taking psychotropic medications, the drugs begin to change the way you feel. Much of your mind is distracted by the adaptations your mind has to make for the new chemicals. During this temporary period, judgment is not always good. Whatever you decide to do, be patient and talk over your plans with your doctor *before* you carry them out.

Q-70. My hands shake a lot and my mouth quivers when I get angry. Is this normal for people on medication?

Some drugs, especially lithium, cause shakiness or tremor especially noticeable in the hands. When I get excited, nervous, angry, or emotional, this shakiness occurs and increases in proportion to the level of my emotions. If I am the center of attention in a small crowd of people, they notice the shaking of my hands first and the quivering of my mouth muscles second. When I first notice shakiness happening, I focus on my hands or facial muscles and try to stop the side effect; it works sometimes. Most people who take medications such as lithium have to tolerate a mild shakiness now and then, but your doctor could prescribe propranolol (Inderal) or another similar drug to reduce the shakiness. I recommend discussing your symptoms and options with your doctor. If you have severe shakiness or tremor, you should let your doctor know immediately.

Q-71. I have been on medication for my illness for over a year. Sometimes I think I feel the edge of the illness again. Am I imagining things?

No. Medication restrains the manic or depressive episode, but you may still feel it's fringes. Let me give you an imaginative illustration that helps me understand and answer your question.

Before you were on medication, a "wild animal" called bipolar disorder was allowed to roam through your mind and emotions wreaking destruction on your mental health. Through medication, that "wild animal" is now being held captive by an elastic "fence" called medication, and the "animal" can no longer roam about and wreck your mental health. At times, with or without medication, the "animal" may decide to sleep for a while, and we feel no sign of the illness. But sometimes the "wild animal" tries to make its presence known by ramming the fence and deflecting the fence in an attempt to get out. This is when you feel the "edge" of a severe mood disturbance that is being restrained by medication and when you actually feel a "restraining force." At other times, the "wild animal" sticks its head over the fence in an attempt to get out. This is when your medication is partially effective and some minor symptoms return, not a full manic or depressive episode. If a full manic or depressive episode occurs, the "wild animal" has broken down the fence and gotten out again. The hope for all people with this illness is to construct an adequate, durable "fence" of medication so that the "wild animal" will never stick its head over the fence and never break the fence down. And remember, that "wild animal" will be with you all your life, so you must continuously monitor the "fence" (or medications) for a weakness or an inadequacy.

Q-72. A member of our support group takes twice as much of the same medication as I do each day. Isn't he taking too much?

Not necessarily. Because bodies are different, some people require higher dosages to reach an effective concentration in their blood as compared to yours. For example, one person could take 900 mg of lithium per day while another could take 1,800 mg; both could have the same drug concentration in their blood. In other people, a higher dosage may be required because a medication isn't effective at a lower dosage. You probably will find that medications and dosages vary significantly among people with bipolar illness. Although a comparison of medications and their effectiveness may be beneficial to you, a comparison of dosages won't tell you if the dosage is too high or too low for a particular person.

Q-73. My doctor has me arbitrarily taking a double dose of my medication in the morning and a single dose at night. I don't feel well in the morning after taking the double dose. In general, is there a better way to distribute my medications?

I can identify with your desire to space out medications evenly in a 24-hour period. I try to avoid having spikes or periods of higher medication concentration in my system. I am very sensitive to psychotropic medications, and I can feel or sense even the smallest changes in dosages or fluctuations in the concentration of drugs in my blood. Although this may appear as a minor benefit in my treatment, I feel a little better when a peak is leveled off.

The rules about when to take medications are many, and I can't give you a simple solution to your problem. Some medications should be taken only in the morning and some only before going to bed. To minimize side effects during the day, some types require a smaller dose in the morning with a larger dose at night. Others can't be taken with certain types of foods. For some types of medications, taking too much at one time can cause a toxic concentration in your blood. In all these cases, special problems and restrictions arise in the attempt to redistribute your medications in a 24-hour period. Therefore, your specific medication must be evaluated. Here are several things you can do to get an answer to your problem:

1. Tell your doctor about your problem, and ask for a new medication schedule or another solution to your problem.
2. Ask your pharmacist for advice.
3. Read the product information sheet that comes with your prescription; if you don't have it, ask your pharmacist for a copy. Read the sheet and search for recommended dosage schedules.

Your doctor may want you taking larger dosages at certain times of the day for a particular reason; however, dosages at particular times could be arbitrary. If you are considering a change in the time you take your medications, discuss your options with your doctor before making a change.

Q-74. Why do people discontinue their medications?

The biggest and most obvious reason for discontinuing a medication is that the drug doesn't help sufficiently in relieving depression, mania, or psychosis. This happens because a particular drug can have varying degrees of success in reducing symptoms of the illness. Some drugs aren't effective at all on some individuals. The whole process of finding a satisfactory drug is a trial-and-error approach, and when one medication is cast aside, another one usually is tried.

Rejecting a drug because of the side effects is also common. Many people don't like the weight gain, shakiness of the hands, dizziness, nausea, or some other effect. Sometimes life-threatening side effects occur that require discontinuing a drug.

After being on medication(s) for some time, a person with bipolar illness usually feels much better. Some individuals think that since they feel great, they have been cured, and no longer need the medication. After discontinuing their medication, they may not have an *immediate* return of symptoms, thus reinforcing their decision to go off of medication. Perhaps a few weeks or months pass by, and mania, depression, or psychosis may return because no medication is available in their bodies.

Q-75. I don't like my medication. How do I go off of it?

After reviewing with your doctor the side effects and the effectiveness of the medication, you could decide to stop using a particular medication. Almost every person with bipolar illness treated with medications has experienced going off of a medication as part of the trial-and-error process involved in finding the right drug(s).

Your doctor will tell you the necessary rate of withdrawal from a drug. If you abruptly stop a medication against your doctor's advice, you are likely to experience severe and distressing side effects depending on the medication type and dosage. Remember, these drugs are powerful, and our minds can take only so much change. So always use mature, sound judgment and think things through when going off a medication.

Q-76. If I keep going on and off my medications, will that reduce their effectiveness?

In my bipolar support group, I heard that some research has indicated that the effectiveness of lithium *may* be decreased by repeated cycles of going on and off of the drug. Other medications used to treat bipolar illness could be similarly affected, but there hasn't been a lot of research on this to know one way or the other.

I know several people with bipolar illness who begin their medication when they feel symptoms of depression or mania and end medication sometime later. They do this because they can't stand the side effects of their drug(s), particularly weight gain.

If you know that you eventually will have another manic or depressive episode, why do you want to risk being without medication in your system? You know that once an episode begins, it takes a while for medication(s) to reach a therapeutic level, and the unrestrained beginning of an episode is likely to be very disruptive in your life. Is doing away with the drug due to side effects a fair trade for a return of symptoms and possible hospitalization? What would you do if the only drug that worked for you became ineffective due to cycles of going on and off of the drug? If you remain on the medication from the beginning, you won't have to worry whether going on and off of your medication will reduce its effectiveness or not.

Q-77. Will I be able to continue at my current medication dosage throughout my ife?

Not necessarily. I used to think that because I've been stable for several years at a certain dosage of medication that it always will be that way; however, things can change.

Early in June, 1993, I noticed that I was starting to sleep over an hour more than usual, and I thought it was due to being tired from stress. My motivation and energy level had dropped some, and I thought it was just temporary. Several weeks passed by, and I started waking up depressed; this was very rare for me. Several days passed when I felt normal and good. Then I noticed that I was thinking too much about things, and I couldn't stop the thoughts. I couldn't sleep well, and I woke up with my thoughts already going "90 mph." Then it occurred to me that partial symptoms of my bipolar illness had returned. But how? I assumed that my lithium level was stable at 0.6 mEq/l; when I went to my doctor and had a lithium level taken, it was 0.5 mEq/l. For over five years, I knew that a level of 0.6 mEq/l meant that I had no symptoms. Exactly one year ago my lithium level had dropped to 0.5 mEq/l, and I had increased my lithium dosage from 900 mg/day to 1,012 mg/day. What had caused my medication needs to change two years in a row? Was it caused by the summer heat, changes in the way my body uses lithium, my two-mile walks, my diet, or my drinking a lot of water? Perhaps some of these were the cause. Right away I increased my lithium dosage to 1,125 mg/day from 1,012 mg/day, and my symptoms vanished as soon as my lithium level went back to 0.6 mEq/l.

You may need to adjust your dosage over time, and there isn't any way to predict when this time is approaching. With close monitoring of your medication levels and their effectiveness, you and your doctor can make the necessary adjustments quickly as needed. If you experience the slightest bit of symptoms and feel that this is abnormal for you, contact your doctor and find out why.

Q-78. Should I keep an extra supply of medication around?

First, I suggest that you maintain (at home) at least a 10-day supply of your medication(s) at all times, and never let your supply run down to a few doses. If your prescription is almost out and your doctor is on vacation, a renewal may be difficult. A natural disaster such as an earthquake, hurricane, tornado, flood, or blizzard could hinder your efforts to get a prescription renewed when you need it. The quantity of 10 days is a minimum and should be adjusted upwards depending on the types of disasters that are possible in your area.

Or, what would you do if your residence burned down and all your medication was destroyed? If you are employed, store a five-day medicine supply at your workplace. What if your car broke down, and you couldn't get home tonight? You could keep a five-day supply in your car, but watch out for heat sensitive medications. Another solution is keeping a five-day supply on "your person."

If you are on a trip, take enough medication for the whole trip plus a 10-day supply in case something happens. I recommend splitting the medication up and putting it in different suitcases or garment bags. For an added precaution while traveling, you could carry an extra prescription for each of your medications. However, you could lose the prescriptions or have them stolen, so find the safest place to keep medication, such as in the map pouches of the car or in something that you won't let out of your sight. Finally, you might want to bring your doctor's phone number with you, give it to a friend, or memorize it.

Q-79. If I'm in an accident, how will the rescue people know which medications I'm on?

If you are in an accident, or for some reason rendered unconscious, rescue and medical personnel need to know what medications are already in your system. If you need an emergency operation, the anesthesiologist needs to know your medications. For a doctor to use certain drugs to help you, that doctor must know how new medications react with the medications already in your body. Therefore, a very important procedure is to have some sort of medical identification, and the following 10 items are necessary for thorough identification:

1. Your full name.
2. Your home address if not already on other identification.
3. Your home phone number.
4. Doctor's name.
5. Doctor's phone number(s).
6. Medication name(s).
7. Quantity of medication(s).
8. Normal time of day you take it.
9. Date you first started taking the dosage(s) in item 7 above.
10. All the names of your illnesses or disorders (e.g., bipolar disorder, panic disorder, etc.)

One solution is wearing a medical identification bracelet. Check with your doctor or pharmacist to find out where to get one.

My choice is to keep a waterproof identification card with me at all times. The 10 items above can be typed on an index card or piece of paper, about the same size as a credit card, and then laminated with plastic. The plastic laminate can be purchased at most office supply stores. You might want to include the names and phone numbers of friends and relatives on the other side of the card. When any information changes, be sure to update the card.

Another source of medical information in case of an emergency is the Medication Identification Vial. To make one, take one of your empty medication bottles or containers, and place the information (items 1–10 above) in it. Label the container with the words, "Medication Identification," and include your full name on the outside. Place the container in the same place as all your other medications.

Q-80. Sometimes I do not recall whether or not I've taken my medicine. How can I remember to take it regularly?

I found that a pill box helped greatly. I bought mine for several dollars at an ordinary drug store. My box is divided into one compartment for each day of the week, and some boxes have bigger daily compartments for larger amounts of medicine. I make it a weekly practice of refilling my box with a week's supply every Saturday night after I take Saturday night's dose. Then I put the small pill box in the bathroom sink. Every morning and night I have to physically remove it from the sink to brush my teeth, and I see it every time I go into the bathroom. Then I'm reminded of the need to check if I've taken my pill(s). I'm sure you'll find a pill box very helpful (especially when travelling). Also, putting the pill container in a location that you'll encounter in your daily schedule is necessary. I also take a pill at 5:00p.m. every day, and I use an alarm watch to remind me. In the six years that I have been taking pills, I have missed only one night's dosage.

Q-81. If I'm pregnant, will my medications cause trouble for me and my unborn baby?

For most of the medications used to treat bipolar disorder, there are varying degrees of risk to the fetus for birth defects. For some medications such as lithium carbonate, there is actual evidence of risk to the human fetus. For other medications, adverse effects to the fetus have been shown only in animal studies. Some medications are harmful during certain times of development of the fetus, while others may be detrimental all the time.

If you discover that you are pregnant, go to your doctor immediately and discuss the effect of your medications on your unborn baby. You may have to go off some or all of your medications, and this must be done under your doctor's careful supervision. Going off of any medication may cause your bipolar symptoms to reappear; so you may have some difficult times. Your doctor will help you work out a plan that minimizes the risks to you and your unborn baby.

For all those who are thinking about getting pregnant, discuss medication issues thoroughly with your doctor. I suggest that you get a drug handbook and look up the medications that you are taking. Talking to your pharmacist and reading the drug manufacturer's leaflet on your medication can be enlightening and reassuring too.

Q-82. Will medications affect my ability to obtain an airplane pilot's license, truck driver's license, or automobile driver's license?

The psychotropic medications used to treat bipolar illness cause side effects such as an inability to concentrate or drowsiness, and these are sufficient to impair a person's ability to operate an airplane, truck, or automobile. Although some people have no significant impairment from medication, all those taking a particular medication are grouped together and suffer the same consequences (e.g., denial of a license) for taking the medication whether or not side effects are present.

According to the Flight Surgeon's Office of the Federal Aviation Administration, the use of any psychotropic medications used to treat bipolar illness will exclude you from getting or keeping an aircraft pilot's license. For further information, call the FAA; look in the phone book in the government pages under United States Government Offices, Transportation Department of, Federal Aviation Administration, Flight Standards.

If you take medications for bipolar illness and want to obtain a commercial license to drive trucks, in most every case, you will be denied a license. If you have been driving trucks for a number of years and later get diagnosed *and* medicated for bipolar illness, your right to keep your commercial license would be evaluated on a case by case basis. If you take "substantial" medication, you probably will not be permitted keep your license. I haven't found any regulations prohibiting the use of psychotropic medications for automobile drivers. For both trucks and automobiles, I recommend that you check the specific laws where you live. For further information, look in the phone book in the government pages under State Government Offices, Motor Vehicles Department, Driver Safety Section.

PR-4. A PSYCHIATRIST'S RESPONSE

The essence of a good medication program for a patient with bipolar disorder is to have a physician who is knowledgeable and willing to communicate his knowledge and expertise about the medications used. I am pleased when a patient is shy and even suspicious of taking medication for an emotional or psychological disorder. Such a patient nearly always responds to adequate information and honest answers to all questions. I am far more uncomfortable with patients who come asking for medication, with the hopes that the medication will solve their problems or symptoms without effort or pain. These individuals tend to seek out medications that are rapid in action, completely remove the symptoms, and even produce a feeling of euphoria. These medications are always addictive and are rarely indicated for individuals who have a bipolar disorder.

Several medications are now used to treat the symptoms of bipolar disorder, and the success rate is very high. In fact, the medication regimen for bipolar disorder forms the very backbone of the treatment program.

Medications are used not only for the treatment of bipolar disorder but also for the prevention of recurrences. The goal of any successful treatment program must include prevention as well as relief from the many serious symptoms of bipolar disorder.

USE OF LITHIUM CARBONATE

Q-83. What is lithium carbonate?

Lithium and lithium carbonate are not fancy designer drugs fashioned by modern chemistry; they occur in nature. The element lithium is found everywhere on Earth in trace amounts, but the lithium we have as medication is mined from rocks. Lithium carbonate is a molecule composed of two atoms of lithium, one atom of carbon, and three atoms of oxygen. When this molecule enters water, the lithium atom separates from the molecule and is able to move freely in our bodily fluids. The lithium atom substitutes for what is missing in the brain chemistry of people with bipolar disorder.

Q-84. Prior to the discovery of lithium's antimanic effect in 1949, was there any historical use of lithium to treat this illness?

In the late 1800s, some used "lithia water" that came from springs with a high content of lithium to treat "nervous diseases," and people were advised to drink a *gallon* or more of lithia water per day. Some claimed to be healed of their depression and nervous abnormalities while drinking volumes of lithia water; however, its effectiveness was not clear. There was a crude use of lithium to treat symptoms that we call mania and depression. Contact the Lithium Information Center (see Q-186 for address) for more information on lithium and its medical use.

57

Q-85. How is lithium carbonate given to people today?

Lithium carbonate comes in capsules and tablet form as *Eskalith, Eskalith CR, Lithane, Lithobid, Lithonate,* and *Lithotabs.* Hospitals frequently use a syrup called lithium citrate (*Cibalith-S*) to get lithium into patients faster.

In my experience, I felt a mild side effect as the lithium entered my system after taking two 300mg capsules. I felt a slight nausea for an hour after taking the capsules. I changed the type of lithium medication to the 450mg controlled release tablet, Eskalith CR, and I felt no further symptoms. Furthermore, I was able to cut the 450mg tablet into quarter pieces so that I could take my usual dosage of 2.25 tablets per day. With lithium carbonate in tablet form, I am not restricted to taking multiples of 300mg capsules.

Q-86. What are some initial side effects of lithium?

Initially, most people experience a few of these side effects in a mild way, and the side effects may change to others on the list from week to week. After several weeks, most of the side effects will vanish, but a few may linger in some people.

1. Acne.
2. "Cotton" mouth, dry mouth, "pasty" mouth.
3. Drowsiness.
4. Feeling a little "weird."
5. Increased urination.
6. Irritability.
7. Metallic taste.
8. Nausea.
9. Restlessness.
10. Shakiness in the hands.
11. Thirst.
12. Weakness or fatigue.
13. Weight gain (also a long-term effect).

Q-87. I have been on lithium for a few months and have gained some weight. Is my weight gain all fat?

No. When you absorb lithium, the body's fluid volume increases. Some of this weight gain is actually water weight of about five to seven pounds.

Q-88. Why is a blood test necessary when I take lithium?

Depending on the concentration of lithium in your blood (also called lithium level), lithium can be toxic, poisonous, or even ineffective. The use of lithium is unique as compared to other drugs because the normal helpful dosage is very close to one that could make you sick. For this reason, it must be closely monitored by a blood level test. When you first start taking lithium, you'll have a blood test to measure your lithium level every week until the level of lithium stabilizes. To get an accurate lithium level, check 12 hours after your last dose of lithium. Common practice is to have your blood drawn early in the morning before you eat breakfast and prior to your morning lithium dosage. Depending on your body chemistry and the degree of your bipolar disorder, a lithium level could be required every month, every other month, or every three months.

Researchers have found that lithium does well in the treatment of mania (and depression) when the concentration of lithium is between 0.6-1.2 mEq/l, but these numbers are not exact for everyone. Generally, if the lithium level is over 1.2 mEq/l, a person will develop symptoms of toxicity. (The units, mEq/l, stand for milliequivalents per liter and are a measure of the concentration of lithium per unit blood serum volume.) If the level is under 0.6 mEq/l, some partial symptoms return, and this is reliable for most people on lithium. For a few, lithium levels in the 0.4 to 0.6 mEq/l range are effective; others develop some toxic side effects at 1.0 or 1.1 mEq/l.

Because the upper end of the lithium level range approaches toxicity, many doctors like to keep their patients in the lower part of that range. Also, side effects due to lithium will be less with a lower lithium level. Some, however, must go to a 1.0 or 1.1 because lithium has not been effective in treating their symptoms at the lower part of the range.

Q-89. While I am on lithium, are there regular tests that I need performed other than a lithium level?

The minimum recommendations for monitoring the effects of lithium are to have the following tests done:

1. thyroid function, (T_4, Free T_4, TSH), every six months;
2. kidney (renal) function (creatinine), every six months;
3. complete blood count including white blood cells, every 6 to 12 months; and

Q-90. Are there some medications that have adverse interactions with lithium?

Yes. Here is a partial list of medications known to cause adverse interactions with lithium. Many of these drugs can raise or lower a person's lithium level, and the reactions range from minor to severe depending on the individual and the dosage.

> Advil, Aprozide, Azolid, Bronkaid, Butazolidin, Capoten, Capozide, Chlorzide, Constant-T, Diaqua, Diuril, Dyazide, Esidrix, Feldene, HydroDIURIL, Hydromal, Hydropres, Hydro-Z-50, Hyperetic, Indocin, Marax, Maxzide, Medipren, Midol, Motrin, Mudrane, Naprosyn, Nuprin, Oretic, Ponstel, Primatene, Prinivil, Quibron, Respbid, Ro-Hydrazide, Rufen, SK-Hydrochlorothiazide, Slo-Phyllin, Sustaire, Theo-Dur, Theospan-SR, Trendar, Vasotec, and Zestril.

There are other medications, both prescription and non-prescription, that would make a lithium user sick. If you have any questions about your specific medication, consult your doctor and your pharmacist. Also, it's very important that you read a related question, Q-64.

Q-91. I heard that if I lose a lot of body fluids, my lithium level will go up. Is this true?

Yes. If you lose a lot of water, the concentration of lithium in your body will rise. If it goes too high, you could reach intoxication with lithium. The following can contribute or cause your lithium level to rise:

1. excessive sweating due to heat, exercise, saunas, and steam rooms;
2. dehydration;
3. some blood pressure medicines that remove fluid from your body;
4. medicines that are diuretics;
5. drinking a lot of tea; and/or
6. prolonged vomiting.
7. Persistent diarrhea.

Q-92. How do I know if I am toxic with Lithium?

If you have reached intoxication, your lithium level has gone too high. You would experience some or many of the following symptoms of intoxication:

1. apathy;
2. blurred vision;
3. confusion, difficult to concentrate;
4. diarrhea;
5. difficulty in walking;
6. dizziness;
7. frequent muscle twitching;
8. irregular heart beat;
9. nausea, vomiting;
10. severe shakiness of the hands;
11. slurred speech;
12. swelling of the feet or lower legs; and/or
13. weakness.

If you have some of these symptoms, call your doctor immediately. If your intoxication to lithium continues to get worse, you could fall into a coma, have brain damage, or die. Do not hesitate to get help. If you can not reach a doctor, go to the emergency room of a hospital; this is something you should not put off until tomorrow.

PR-5. A PSYCHIATRIST'S RESPONSE

The medications used to treat bipolar disorder include mood stabilizers such as lithium, valproate (valproic acid), and carbamazepine (Tegretol). Neuroleptic (tranquilizing) drugs such as chlorpromazine (Thorazine) and haloperidol (Haldol) have been used primarily for adjunctive therapy (an addition to other treatment efforts) of mania, but recent guidelines encourage the use of benzodiazepines (drugs producing sedative and hypnotic effects) instead of the neuroleptics. Antidepressants also are often used together with a mood stabilizer, but they must be prescribed with caution because of their tendency to precipitate mania in bipolar patients.

Lithium and benzodiazepines currently are considered to be the most appropriate medications for treatment of the manic phase of bipolar disorder. Lithium is almost 80% effective, and neuroleptics are almost as useful. But because of the neuroleptic's tendency to cause serious side effects, benzodiazepines are now preferred. The combination of lithium and benzodiazepines has proven to be quite effective and reasonably safe; however, close monitoring of the patient's symptoms is highly advisable.

Lithium has a slower onset of action because it takes 7 to 12 days to take effect in highly disturbed patients. Therefore, most physicians have favored beginning treatment of acute mania with a very potent antipsychotic such as halo-peridol (Haldol) to gain quick control of the symptoms. Benzodiazepines, how-ever, are frequently as effective as neuroleptics for adjunctive treatment of mania and do not pose a risk of extrapyramidal symptoms (neurologic distur-bances) such as tardive diskinesia common to neuroleptics. The use of clon-azepam (Klonopin), a benzodiazepine, in dosages of 2 to 4 milligrams four times a day is found to be rapid in effect and well tolerated in controlling acute mania.

After two weeks of adequate plasma lithium levels, if an outpatient does not respond to lithium alone, hospitalization is probably necessary to determine why the patient is not responding. If hospitalization is not possible, neuroleptics such as Haldol, Thorazine, or the benzodiazepines should be considered alone or in combination with lithium.

Physicians generally believe that patients with bipolar disorder should re-main on lithium indefinitely. Lithium is the drug of choice for maintenance treatment, and the dosage should be decreased to the lowest level required for continued efficacy. Lithium is not used during the first three or four months of pregnancy because it has the potential to cause serious effects to the unborn baby. If lithium is absolutely indicated, it may be reinstituted and adjusted ac-cordingly for the last five months of the pregnancy, but it must be monitored carefully. The dosage of lithium should be decreased or discontinued a few days before and after delivery to protect the kidneys. Breast feeding should be strongly discouraged because lithium is excreted in the mother's milk, and there is not a lot of information regarding lithium's effect on the systems of a devel-oping infant.

USE OF OTHER MEDICATIONS

Q-93. Are there any other drugs used to treat mania?

Although lithium carbonate is the drug of first choice for treating mania, it is not effective in treating all people. Some are helped partially or not at all, and others have unacceptable side effects from lithium. The addition of one of the following three mood stabilizers has been helpful in getting lithium to be more effective: carbamazepine, clonazepam, and valproic acid. If lithium is not used to treat someone with bipolar disorder, generally one of the following three drugs would be used. These are actually classified as anticonvulsants, but they are known to be beneficial in treating mania. From the experiences of those at my 1992 support group, carbamazepine is used more often than valproic acid, and clonazepam is rarely used; but usages are changing. If you want to know more about carbamazepine and valproic acid, both the Lithium Information Center and the National Depressive and Manic-Depressive Association have excellent materials available on them (see Q-186 and Q-139 respectively for addresses). Furthermore, I recommend that you research these drugs, if you are taking them, and find out what the regular laboratory tests are for monitoring your health while taking these drugs.

Chemical Name (Manufacturer's Name)

1. Carbamazepine (Epitol, Mazepine, Tegretol)
2. Clonazepam (Klonopin, Rivotril)
3. Valproic acid (Depakene) and sodium valproate (Depakote)

Q-94. Why do some people take antidepressants in addition to mood stabilizers?

In many with bipolar disorder, lithium, carbamazepine, and valproic acid have not been 100% effective in treating depressive episodes, but many experience a partial reduction in symptoms. If this remaining depression is not due to other medical problems, it is common to add an antidepressant to reduce or hopefully eliminate depression.

For the first year that I was on medication, I took lithium carbonate alone, and I never felt depressed or had hypomanic symptoms. I worked part-time for four hours every morning because I didn't have the energy to work an eight-hour day and do all the chores that I needed to do at home. After I left work, I went home and fixed lunch. Within an hour, I felt very drowsy, and I usually fell asleep for an hour or two. Then the rest of the day was a low energy day, and I felt sluggish most of the time. I didn't have the typical feelings of sadness or despair associated with depression, but *my energy level was depressed* or lower than normal. This wasn't the kind of life I wanted; it was just an existence.

My doctor suggested that I try an antidepressant in addition to lithium. After going through the trial-and-error approach of selecting a suitable antidepressant, I found one that eliminated that slow, dull, sluggish feeling. Within several months, I had increased my work hours to 40 hours per week. Eventually, I changed jobs to a more demanding one, and I was able to work "full-speed" for a 40-hour work week. In fact, I performed better than most of the other employees.

Q-95. What are some of the common antidepressants?

The following list contains many of the antidepressants used to treat depression. These antidepressants are not recommended to be used in someone with bipolar illness unless a mood stabilizer or antimanic agent also is used. Adverse side effects may occur when taking some of these antidepressants in combination with lithium, carbamazepine, valproic acid, and clonazepam as well as other psychotropic drugs and even some foods. Drug interactions should be thoroughly researched prior to the addition of an antidepressant. Some antidepressants have additional beneficial effects such as suppressing anxieties, phobias, and obsessive-compulsive behavior, to name a few.

Sometimes doctors give medications to patients without giving the patient any information about the drug's purpose; then these patients ask members of a support group for this information. Hopefully, the following list will speed up the process and let patients know what kind of medication they take. This list is to be used as a quick reference to determine the type of medication you're taking, and further reading on your specific antidepressant medication in a good drug handbook is encouraged.

Heterocyclic Antidepressants (formerly called Tricyclics)
Chemical Name (Manufacturer's Name)

1. Amitriptyline hydrochloride (Amitriptyline, Elavil, Emitrip, Endep, Enovil, SK-Amitriptyline)
2. Amoxapine (Asendin)
3. Clomipramine hydrochloride (Anafranil)
4. Desipramine hydrochloride (Norpramin, Pertofrane)
5. Doxepin hydrochloride (Adapin, Sinequan)
6. Imipramine hydrochloride (Janimine, SK-Pramine, Tofranil, Typramine) Imipramine pamoate (Tofranil-PM)
7. Maprotiline hydrochloride (Ludiomil)
8. Nortriptyline hydrochloride (Aventyl, Pamelor)
9. Protriptyline hydrochloride (Triptil, Vivactil)
10. Trimipramine maleate (Surmontil)

Monoamine Oxidase Inhibitor (MAOI) Antidepressants
Chemical Name (Manufacturer's Name)

11. Isocarboxazid (Marplan)
12. Pargyline hydrochloride (Eutonyl)
13. Phenelzine sulfate (Nardil)
14. Tranylcypromine sulfate (Parnate)

Other Antidepressants
Chemical Name (Manufacturer's Name) [Pharmacologic Classification]

15. Bupropion hydrochloride (Wellbutrin) [aminoketone]
16. Fluoxetine hydrochloride (Prozac) [serotonin reuptake inhibitor]
17. Paroxetine hydrochloride (Paxil) [serotonin reuptake inhibitor]
18. Sertraline hydrochloride (Zoloft) [serotonin reuptake inhibitor]
19. Trazodone hydrochloride (Desyrel, Trialodine) [triazolopyridine derivative]

Q-96. Do antidepressants cause rapid cycling?

Certain antidepressants, tricyclics, may bring on or aggravate rapid cycling, and low dosages are a must to prevent this effect; however, antidepressants may not be the only contributing factor. The following are three theories or possible causes for rapid cycling where antidepressants aren't the cause: biological rhythm disturbances, hypothyroidism, and kindling or sensitization. To begin to understand the effects of antidepressants and these three factors on rapid cycling, read *In Bipolar Illness: Rapid Cycling & Its Treatment* (National Depressive and Manic-Depressive Association, 1991). Also, see Q-26 for a related question on rapid cycling.

Q-97. What are some of the common drugs used to treat psychosis?

The following list contains many of the antipsychotic drugs used to treat psychosis. As with all medications, antipsychotics vary in their effectiveness, side effects, and interactions with other medications. This list is to be used as a quick reference to determine the type of medication you're taking, and further reading on your specific antipsychotic medication in a good drug handbook is encouraged. In this list, variants of the same base chemical are due to the drug being supplied as a capsule, tablet, syrup, or for an injection.

Antipsychotic Drugs
Chemical Name (Manufacturer's Name)

1. Acetophenazine maleate (Tindal)
2. Chlorprothixene (Taractan)
3. Chlorpromazine hydrochloride (Chlorzine, Ormazine, Promapar, Promaz, Sonazine, Thorazine, Thor-Prom)
4. Clozapine (Clozaril)
5. Fluphenazine decanoate (Prolixin Decanoate)
   Fluphenazine enanthate (Prolixin Enanthate)
   Fluphenazine hydrochloride (Permitil Hydrochloride, Prolixin Hydrochloride)
6. Haloperidol (Haldol)
   Haloperidol decanoate (Haldol Decanoate)
   Haloperidol lactate (Haldol, Haldol Concentrate)
7. Loxapine hydrochloride (Loxitane C, Loxitane I.M.)
   Loxapine succinate (Loxitane)
8. Mesoridazine besylate (Serentil)
9. Molindone hydrochloride (Moban)

10. Perphenazine (Trilafon)
    Perphenazine and amitriptyline hydrochloride (Etrafon, Triavil)
11. Pimozide (Orap)
12. Piperacetazine (Quide)
13. Prochlorperazine (Compazine)
    Prochlorperazine edisylate (Compazine)
    Prochlorperazine maleate (Chlorazine, Compazine, Compazine Spansule)
14. Reserpine (Sandril, Serpalan, Serpanray, Serpasil, Serpate, Zepine)
15. Thioridazine (Mellaril-S)
    Thioridazine hydrochloride (Mellaril, Millazine)
16. Thiothixene (Navane)
    Thiothixene hydrochloride (Navane)
17. Trifluoperazine hydrochloride (Stelazine, Suprazine)
18. Triflupromazine (Vesprin)

Q-98. What is Cogentin?

Cogentin is a drug used to counteract movement side effects and muscle rigidity caused by antipsychotic medications such as Haldol. Cogentin is called an antiparkinsonian agent, and its chemical name is benztropine mesylate.

A second antiparkinsonian agent, similar to Cogentin, is trihexyphenidyl hydrochloride, and the manufacturers' names for this chemical are: Aphen, Artane, Artane Sequels, Tremin, Trihexane, Trihexidyl, Trihexy-2, and Trihexy-5.

PR-6. A PSYCHIATRIST'S RESPONSE

A common belief is that hypomanic or depressive episodes should be treated aggressively treated and every effort be made to prevent them from recurring. If these pathological episodes are intense and allowed to be prolonged, they tend to occur more frequently and become more severe over the years. If the physician can aggressively treat and then prevent recurrences, the long-term prognosis is much better than for those patients who have repeated, intense recurrence of debilitating symptoms.

Neuroleptics such as haloperidol (Haldol) and chlorpromazine (Thorazine) have been used in place of, or in addition to, lithium particularly in the treatment of mania. They are used less now because of their side effects, particularly tardive dyskinesia, which causes permanent and unpleasant motor tics (movements) about the face and mouth.

New guidelines recently issued by the American Psychiatric Association state that valproate (valproic acid) and carbamazepine (Tegretol) may be prescribed for patients who prefer these drugs' side effects or who cannot take lithium, cannot tolerate it, or do not respond to it. Experts say that these drugs have been underutilized by American psychiatrists. Generally, they are used as a second line of therapy, but there are some patients for whom valproate as a first line of therapy is recommended including those with mixed features or rapid cycling.

Carbamazepine (Tegretol), an approved anticonvulsive drug, has been found to be quite effective in cases of mania that do not respond well to lithium; however, most physicians prefer not to put their patients at risk for a serious abnormal blood condition, which is a possible side effect of Tegretol. They now prefer to use valproate, which is an effective mood stabilizer for patients unable to tolerate the side effects of lithium. The more common side effects of valproate include weight gain and hair loss, which are not permanent or severe. Valproate is considered a safe and effective medication for the treatment of acute mania as well as a long-term mood stabilizer.

These new guidelines also encourage psychiatrists to prescribe benzodiazepines (drugs producing sedation and hypnotic effects) instead of neuroleptics for manic patients who are receiving mood stabilizers and who require adjunctive therapy (an addition to other treatment efforts). The benzodiazepines now are viewed as effective as neuroleptics for adjunctive treatment of mania yet do not pose a risk of extrapyramidal symptoms (neurologic disturbances) or tardive dyskinesia as neuroleptics do.

The benzodiazepine clonazepam (Klonopin) has been used as an anticonvulsant for several years and is considered safe and useful for acute manic episodes as well as an adjunct to lithium therapy in enhancing early behavioral control. Klonopin is also useful together with lithium in patients who have previously required combined lithium-neuroleptic maintenance regimens. Addiction-prone individuals such as alcoholics or drug addicts should be monitored carefully by their physicians when receiving Klonopin because of the predisposition of such patients to habituation and addiction.

Some patients not only have a bipolar disorder but also may have an anxiety disorder such as a panic disorder or agoraphobia. Many of these patients also need to be on an anxiolytic (anxiety reducing) medication, or a selective serotonin reuptake inhibitor (SSRI), or a heterocyclic antidepressant; all are medications commonly used to help a patient deal with overwhelming anxiety or panic.

Anxiolytics include such medications as Klonopin, Ativan, Librium, Valium, Xanax, Serax, Tranxene, barbiturates; all have the ability to reduce anxiety to tolerable levels. These medications must be monitored very carefully by the physician and viewed with considerable caution and wariness by the patient. One cannot predict when and if addiction or tolerance develops to these anxiety reducing medications. These drugs always should be considered potentially dangerous, and care should be used in taking them. These prescription medications can "sneak up" on oneself and before one knows it, he or she is "hooked."

Generally, the potent, fast-acting anxiolytics such as Xanax, Ativan, and Valium, are the most addicting. Addiction is characterized by symptoms of serious distress when the medication is no longer in one's body. For example, the half-life of Xanax is 12 to 15 hours, and withdrawal symptoms can occur rather quickly. A person addicted to Xanax will begin to feel intense anxiety, aching, nausea, diarrhea, shaky tremor—all very uncomfortable symptoms that tell the physician that the patient is addicted to Xanax and must be withdrawn more slowly. Patients even can be addicted to very low doses of benzodiazepines such as Xanax.

Sometimes it is absolutely necessary for a patient to take anxiety reducing medications. If so, the patient and the doctor must make every effort to find other ways and different medications to lower the anxiety, prevent the panic, and restore the patient to normal mental health without long-term use of these addicting medications.

OTHER TREATMENTS

Q-99. What is ECT, and when is it used?

ECT stands for Electroconvulsive Therapy, and it includes giving a small electric charge to the body to make the person convulse for a few minutes. ECT is done in a hospital for people who are at the extremes of mania and depression when medications are not effective in treatment. For a person who is clearly suicidal, waiting for several weeks for the positive effects of medications is not reasonable. For a person who is severely manic, a rapid end to mania is desirable as the person may suffer from exhaustion. ECT provides quick relief and usually results in the end of a depressive or manic episode, but it may leave the person with little memory of the events around the time of the ECT.

Q-100. Will light therapy help in my treatment for depression?

Some people with bipolar illness report that their depressions and manias follow a seasonal pattern. Winter depressions followed by summer hypomanias occur in some, and spring and fall depressions are typical for some with summer manias. For those individuals with a bipolar disorder who have this seasonal tendency, a supersensitivity to light may exist. Adding artificial light in place of sunlight during the winter has proven to be a beneficial treatment in some suffering from depression, and a better understanding of bipolar disorder is likely to come from treatment studies for those with a seasonal mood pattern.

Light therapy, or phototherapy, involves absorbing light several times brighter than that of an indoor environment from bright lights several feet away. The amount of light varies from half an hour to several hours, and the benefit of the light therapy comes through the eyes and not the skin. The optimum dosage and wavelength of light are not yet known. Some think that the light should be applied before dawn in an attempt to increase the perceived length of daylight. Others have found light therapy in the middle of the day is just as effective.

In general, living and working in a bright environment is good advice for everybody. I also think that going outside midday, even if it is freezing, for a walk in the sunlight during winter is another helpful form of light therapy.

PR-7. A PSYCHIATRIST'S RESPONSE

In the first few months of my training as a psychiatrist, I was assigned as a patient a young man who was catatonic and unable to drink, eat, or even void. The senior psychiatrist on the ward decided he should be treated with electroshock treatments and ordered me to carry them out. I was appalled. I did not "believe in" ECT and told him that it was a relic of the days of "One Flew Over the Cuckoo's Nest." My supervisor looked coldly at me and said, "When you know something about ECT, I will listen to your objections—do it."

So, I found out how to do ECT and administered it to the young man. I was amazed at how quickly and effectively it worked. Within a very short period of time he was wide awake, alert, talking to me, and responding appropriately. That one experience changed my attitudes and beliefs about ECT, and I no longer objected to it. In private practice, however, I seldom have found it necessary to use ECT other than for those few depressions that did not respond to antidepressant medication and therapy.

ECT is a "life saver" for manic patients who cannot be controlled quickly with medications. It should never be withheld from a patient when it is indicated, and I find it a humane and totally appropriate treatment modality when indicated.

Section **8**

FAITH AND ATTITUDE

Q-101. My attitude stinks, and I don't like it. How can I change my attitude?

If you have a bad attitude about something, ask yourself if you can change the situation or problem. Take action if you can, but most of the time you'll have to live with the external environment as it is. Your attitude is your reaction to your own beliefs, and your beliefs can be changed. So change your thoughts and beliefs, and your attitude will change. If you choose to believe that your life is over, that you have no future, that no one will like you, or that you are somehow defective, you will have a sad, bitter attitude. If you choose to believe, however, that you count in this world, that some people will be attracted to you and appreciate you for what you've been through, that you have an illness but you as a person aren't flawed, and that your future is what you make it with the resources you possess, your attitude will be positive, optimistic, and dynamic. Only you can change your attitude by changing your beliefs, and that makes attitude a choice!

Q-102. I recently have been diagnosed with bipolar disorder. I still have symptoms, and I don't like the side effects of my medication. I am not satisfied with my life in general, and I would rather sit at home and forget everything. What's wrong?

You sound as if nothing is working right in your life. I used to feel that way too. Around the time of my diagnosis with bipolar illness, I was overwhelmed by the complexity of my illness and didn't know how to make my

73

life what I wanted. I was very sure that I was sick and tired of being sick and tired. Then I slowly came to realize that my life is what I make it, and no one else but me can change it. So I got mad at my circumstances and began to change the things I could. I wanted to learn how to love myself and give myself the best, and I knew this would be a process. Over a period of time, I developed some guidelines or activities for improving my life that continue to help me live with my illness.

1. Make a project or business out of improving my mental health, and force myself to spend some time each day on that project.
2. Spend time searching for solutions. If I don't, I won't get any results. What I get out of this process is proportional to what I put into it.
3. Identify the areas of my life that I want to improve and set some realistic goals.
4. Focus my energy on one particular problem or shortcoming or inadequacy or void until I have a solution. Don't spread myself too thin.
5. Focus on what my *abilities* are, not on what my disabilities are.
6. Don't be a perfectionist. Just get the job done in an average manner.
7. Don't resign myself to defeat; never give up.
8. Make a 100% commitment to improving my life. Partial commitments get partial results.
9. Develop a positive attitude and do everything possible to keep it.
10. Work on my "inner" environment and let the "outer" environment take care of itself.
11. Face my fears with courage, and do the things I fear to do.

Here are some areas in the life of a typical person with bipolar illness that potentially need some work, and each requires action on your part *if* they apply to you.

1. If your doctor is not right for you, you should make the effort to choose another.
2. If your support group is less than adequate, search for another.
3. If you don't know much about the illness, find some books and start reading.
4. If your medications are ineffective or if the side effects are unacceptable, work with your doctor and try other medications.
5. If you lack a social life, learn what you must do to make the kind of friends whom you have always wanted.
6. If relationships need improvement, work on them.
7. If you don't like the appearance of your body, really make an effort to improve the things you can.

Each day there is something of value to be learned,
recognized, appreciated, and absorbed into our lives,
and only we can choose to do it.

Q-103. I think constantly about the good physical and mental shape that I was in before this illness. When I think of the shape I'm in today, it makes me very sad. What can I do to help myself out of this?

I think all people with bipolar illness have spent time remembering their accomplishments, strengths, performances, and abilities that occurred in pre-illness days. But doesn't every older person long for the days of youth when they were at their physical peak? Doesn't every person with a long-term illness wish for the return of the days when they were healthy? The answer is yes! This reminiscing might be nice, but does it make you feel good about yourself today? Does it make you feel inadequate, inferior, or damaged?

I have learned that it is fruitless to spend time making comparisons between the "old me" and the "me today." When reminiscing I feel sad and somewhat resentful that I have bipolar disorder. If I make comparisons at all, I make ones that show that some of my abilities are greater today than they were in the past. It is on these greater qualities that I spend my time and attention. We can *choose* to be sad about what we don't have, or we can *choose* to be glad about what we have today. Why should we make ourselves sick living in the past? Since we have only the present, why waste it looking backward?

Q-104. Last week I heard an argument over whether religion or psychiatry had all the answers. What is at the root of this squabble?

For over hundreds or thousands of years, the only ones who were caring for those who were mentally ill were a few in the church; priests and ministers gave encouragement to those who wanted it. However, many atrocities were committed against mentally ill people by the church because no one at that time knew anything about mental illness. Biologically based depression was dealt with as a moral weakness and even a sin. A person who was manic or psychotic often was viewed as demon possessed, and sometimes church members dealt with them cruelly.

Today, mental illness is understood much differently than in the "dark" past. With all the advances in studying the biochemical nature of our moods, some, not the majority, in the psychiatric profession may perceive people as primarily chemical (and psychological) in nature. Thus, some believe that many of our problems are caused by chemical imbalances.

Modern science can give us relief from the symptoms of mental illness, and religion, or spirituality, can answer the "why me" questions and give us the faith to endure until we have a cure. Perhaps neither organized religion nor the psychiatric profession has all the answers independently!

Q-105. Is faith important in recovery?

First, let us explore a definition of faith. Let's say that faith is the belief in something for which there is no proof. Each of my psychiatrists told me that most people of faith do better with bipolar illness than others, and I found faith indispensable. Every time that I was very depressed, I *believed* God would help me through it. When I saw my psychiatrist twice a week, I *believed* that my visits with him were going to alleviate my suffering. Although the answers were nowhere in sight, I *believed* that eventually I would have the solution to my ups and downs. With the uncertainty of my employment picture today, I *believe* that there is a way to make it with or without a job. I *believe* that my talents and abilities have a purpose, and a place for them exists in the future. I strongly *believe* that I'll find friends who will love and accept me just the way I am. I *believe* that I have a future that is worth a great deal. All these beliefs take incredible amounts of faith. Whether your faith is based on your doctor's abilities, a spiritual leader's wisdom, or in a personal relationship with God, these objects of our faith provide a foundation onto which we can hold when the "mighty storm" of bipolar illness rages. Without faith, we may give up or attempt suicide each time we go through a deep depression. Are you strong enough to weather *every* storm on your own? Or do you have faith in Someone to help you when life is confusing and tough? Faith is a major component in successfully living with the illness, and we all have a *choice* in having faith or not. Without faith, is there any hope?

> . . . The Lord is the everlasting God,
> the Creator of the ends of the earth.
> He will not grow tired or weary,
> and his understanding no one can fathom.
> He gives strength to the weary
> and increases the power of the weak.
> Even youths grow tired and weary,
> and young men stumble and fall;
> but those who hope in the Lord
> will renew their strength.
> They will soar on wings like eagles;
> they will run and not grow weary,
> they will walk and not be faint. (Isaiah 39:28-31, *The NIV Bible*)

Q-106. I am well aware of the emotional and physical parts of my identity, but sometimes I am concerned over a lack of anything spiritual in my life. Is a spiritual component necessary?

First, let me say a little about what the word spiritual means to me. Spiritual means relating to, consisting of, or affecting the spirit. What is our spirit? Our spirit is that part of us that gives and sustains life. Without that deeper part of ourselves called our spirit we could not exist. My spirit is different from my emotions, intellect, and physical body, but my spirit has a vital influence on my emotional and physical health. When people discuss their beliefs about something, they say "in my heart" they believe it, not "in their head"; they are describing a separate and distinct spiritual identity. If something isn't quite right in my life and is not due to an emotional or physical problem, it is probably caused by a spiritual one. Spirituality is the soil from which the ideas and important things in life have their roots and beginning.

I am amazed by all the types of religions and faiths that cover all parts of the world. This shows me that man's basic design and need is to have a spiritual identity. Also, all 12-step groups (like Alcoholics Anonymous, etc.) emphasize that we are a three-fold being composed of the physical, the emotional, and the spiritual; these programs realize that recovery from very difficult situations requires a spiritual dimension. Since I am made with a spiritual component to my identity, I must fill it to be a *whole* healthy person.

My spirituality is not the same as following a religion composed of rituals and regulations. Instead, it is a communion with a Person I choose to call God in a real personal relationship. My spirituality is based on trusting in God rather than just believing, and there's a big difference between the two. My spirituality is the foundation or anchor onto which I hold for hope, encouragement, and understanding when I go through turbulent living problems. Without spirituality, I would be lost in the storms of life and maybe even dead.

My spiritual identity gives me a source for answers to questions such as the following:

What is my place in this world?
What is my mission in life?
Who am I?
Why me?

During the days when I ignored the spiritual, I was merely a piece of driftwood going somewhere in life's fast river. But today, my spiritual identity ties me into the rest of the world and the "big picture" of life. I know my reason for living, and without my spiritual identity, I wouldn't know who I am today.

Some with a bipolar disorder have rejected God or distanced themselves from Him because they had a bad experience or can't believe that God would let them suffer as much as they have. Then later in life, they wonder what their purpose is in life, and they try frantically to fill themselves with meaning. Some stop their search for God by inventing a God of their own who endorses all or parts of their self-destructive behavior; that person won't change or grow for the better. From what I have seen in most people with the illness, the weakest part of recovery is their spirituality. If someone wants to become a whole person and fill that empty spot in their life, they must work continually on the spiritual aspects of their life as well as the physical and the emotional. For all those lacking a vibrant spiritual identity, I suggest that they establish their spiritual connection with a fresh, new effort. Everyone whom I have seen who persistently and honestly sought true spirituality eventually found it.

Q-107. Now that I have bipolar illness, I am having a hard time seeing a new purpose for living. What is your purpose for living?

First of all, I believe that I am unique, and I have a special purpose that no one else can fill. I think of myself as a "tool" in God's toolbox. All the experiences that I have been through have shaped and formed me into a special unique instrument for God to use to accomplish His purpose. Here are a few of my purposes in life.

1. Improve my conscious contact with God as I understand Him through prayer and meditation.
2. Seek God's will for my life and let my purpose in life be His purpose. If I continue to do all that I was "meant" to do, I will be satisfied in life.
3. Love everybody (does not mean I have to like everyone's *behavior*).
4. Use my experiences to help others by giving back what I have been given. I have learned that I must give away what I have acquired in order to keep it.
5. Have an attitude of gratitude.
6. Make every day count, and live each to its fullest.

My Grandfather Court had a saying that "if you live life right the first time, once is enough." If I do all of the above to the best of my abilities on a daily basis, I can do no better and will have no regrets when life is over.

Because we have bipolar illness, we shouldn't think that we have a lesser purpose or reason for living; we have our valuable unique experience to give away. If you feel that life has dealt you a lemon, make lemonade. What you make out of your life is up to you.

Here is something to think about. I heard a saying on TV that "the world is filled with wonderful opportunities brilliantly disguised as unsolvable problems," and I thought it applied to bipolar illness. As a result of having bipolar illness, what wonderful opportunities are around the corner and in your future?

Those who succeed are among the ones who try.

PR-8. A PSYCHIATRIST'S RESPONSE

Faith and attitude are a few of the characteristics that make us human, and even the ardent atheist has faith. His or her faith may be different from others who believe in God and participate in an organized religion, but faith is an important aspect of all human beings however it is portrayed. I found that patients with bipolar disorders tend to be bright, inquisitive individuals, who tend to have a lively interest in matters of faith and spirituality.

The patient's faith and trust in his or her physician or therapist is absolutely essential for a good outcome. Attitudes or feelings about therapy and the therapist are matters that should be discussed openly in the therapy sessions. The quality of the therapeutic relationship is one of the most important variables that determines the outcome of the work that a patient and therapist do together. If the patient does not have faith and trust in the therapist, or if the patient has a negative attitude, the outcome of the therapeutic endeavor is at risk.

Furthermore, it is the responsibility of the therapist to engage the patient's attitudes and feelings about the therapeutic process and about the therapist himself or herself. If the patient is reluctant to engage this issue, the therapist is obligated to explore and gently encourage the patient to reveal his or her thoughts and feelings about the process itself.

It is difficult to argue with the success of the 12-step program with its emphasis that participants acknowledge that there is a Higher Power (however named by the faith community to which one belongs) who can restore the patient to normal mental health. I have had several patients who have successfully recovered from their addictive disease tell me reluctantly and sheepishly that "there is something to this Higher Power."

Faith, whether practiced alone or with a faith community, seems to be an important element in the success of any treatment program regardless of diagnosis. This has been my experience with my patients. Faith is an important element in any person's life and becomes increasingly so as the patient grows older. In fact, Carl Jung, a well-known Swiss psychiatrist and contemporary of Sigmund Freud, believed that all patients who became emotionally ill past mid-life were suffering primarily from a spiritual illness characterized by a lack or loss of faith.

ACCEPTANCE

Q-108. I have just started seeing a psychiatrist, and I feel sick about it. Did you experience this too?

For several weeks after I first saw a psychiatrist, I had dreams of people dressed in white trying to lock me up in a mental hospital. I was always running from them as if my life depended on it. I felt sick about my situation, but this is where the beginning of my acceptance of my illness occurred.

For all of my college days, I bragged to myself about how smart I was because I graduated *summa cum laude* with a B.S. degree in civil engineering. I had always enjoyed my intellectual abilities. After several years with bipolar symptoms and no help, I knew I had a problem, but I was sickened when I learned that it was due to a mental illness. I had seen what mentally ill people were like on television (supposedly), and I couldn't accept the idea or fact that I was one of them. To me, being smart and being mentally ill was a contradiction. I took it personally, and I was disappointed in myself because I considered it a weakness.

About a month after beginning therapy, I felt some reassurance because I was feeling a little better. I started basing my feelings on facts rather than long-held perceptions. I started to think that getting help for a problem was a sign of strength and courage. As an engineer, I became comfortable when I knew how and why the illness worked the way it did. I was getting better, and that meant that I had made a good choice in seeing a psychiatrist. If I made good choices,

I didn't need to criticize myself so much. After several weeks of having these kinds of dreams, they ended and never returned.

> Bipolar disorder is a "thorn in my flesh"
> to keep me from being too proud
> about a few significant achievements.

Q-109. Why did God make us this way?

Your question is a tough one, but let me give you my point of view. If God made me with bipolar illness, I would view that as a very sadistic, evil act, and I couldn't live with a God like that. So I choose to believe that my bipolar illness is the result of a genetic defect or perhaps several genes gone bad. I believe that we were all designed by God to have perfectly functioning genes, every last one of them. Some of them have become defective and cause aging and many other diseases in addition to bipolar illness. I believe that God created my spirit, but my body is the product of generations of genetic variation with a beginning in creation (or evolution as others believe). We could believe that our genetic abnormalities were caused by the Fall of Man in the Garden of Eden or by random genetic mutations. In both of these cases, God didn't cause them. Exactly why one or more of my genes have become defective is beyond the scope of human knowledge (and this book). However, God *allowed* us to have bipolar illness, and it is not an accident or defect that caught God by surprise. He knew all about it before we ever set foot on this Earth. Therefore, we must look elsewhere for the reason or purpose in having the illness. Some related questions come to my mind that only you can answer. What good will it do for you to have bipolar illness? How does it affect your mission in life? Answer those questions, and you'll know why God allowed you to have bipolar illness.

> We have nothing to do with the way our life began,
> but we have a lot to do with how it ends.

Q-110. Do you have problems accepting the fact that you have a bipolar disorder?

For almost 10 years, I wrestled with the full symptoms of depression and hypomania, and I often thought that it was unfair or unjust for me to have symptoms for so long. I complained bitterly about life and thought I had been singled out for cruel and unusual punishment. Much of the time I was disappointed because I compared myself to other mentally healthy individuals. I often would reflect on the quality of life before the illness and long to be that person again.

Basically, the problem of acceptance can be summarized as a struggle with the right and wrong of having this illness. When I was diagnosed and treated, I finally knew the cause of the agony I went through. Knowing that the disorder is genetic helped me to quit believing that my illness was some sort of judgment. The knowledge that my illness had a physical origin stopped the accusing voices that condemned me for having a moral or spiritual weakness. Seeing others at a support group helped me to know that I'm not the only person with this disorder, and I can have a life worth living. When I finally gave up the internal fight over whether having the illness was right or wrong, I had reached a higher level of acceptance. With little energy being spent internally on this conflict, I could then concentrate on charting a new path for myself in life.

One of my favorite prayers that helped me separate the things I could change from the things I couldn't is *The Serenity Prayer* often heard at 12-step meetings:

> God, grant me the serenity
> to accept the things I cannot change,
> courage to change the things I can,
> and the wisdom to know the difference.

Q-111. Does bipolar illness erode self-esteem?

For most people it does. Many of us have spent years going through depression and mania not knowing that it was due to bipolar illness. With each mood disturbance, we tried to lift ourselves out of depression or control our manic behavior only to fail in our efforts. Every failure eroded our self-esteem a little more. At the end of all that "erosion" of confidence in ourselves, we felt that we were not worth much since we couldn't do the simple task of managing our emotions.

I spent nine and a half years trying to moderate my moods. I didn't know why I got depressed or hypomanic, but I thought that it was my fault for *staying* in those moods; I tried everything to change the miserable way I felt. One of my "friends" told me that I should read the Bible more, go to church more, and pray more. He said that my mood problems existed because I wasn't trying hard enough. I told him that I was doing all the right things to feel better, but he didn't believe me. Almost everyone I knew made comments similar to his.

All these comments over the nine-and-a-half-year period implied that I didn't have what it took to manage my emotions. I believed the message that others gave me—that I was weak and my character was somehow flawed.

When I finally was diagnosed with bipolar illness, I knew why willpower alone wouldn't keep the mood episodes away; medication alone stopped them almost completely. I stopped blaming myself as others had blamed me. I praised myself for the tremendous courage and long-suffering it took to battle and endure the illness in ignorance without medication. I began to build my self-esteem and make it stronger than before. My confidence came back in time, and my sense of self-satisfaction was renewable. I would once again trust my abilities to make choices concerning my emotional health! Read *Ten Days to Self-Esteem* (Burns, 1993).

> Self-esteem comes back
> as we add our many small successes,
> day after day after day. . . .

Q-112. I miss the way I felt when I was manic. Is this unusual?

No, but let me clarify something. I haven't met too many people who would say they enjoyed the manic episode that got them hospitalized. A manic episode as defined in Q-4 is disabling. I think most people who "mourn" their mania have really experienced hypomania (lower mania) to one degree or another; with hypomania, a person can be fully functional. For some, mania (hypomania) acts like a drug that makes them feel "up," energized, and fully alive. Some people with this illness go through a period of mourning for their mania (hypomania) similar to what a drug addict goes through in the weeks and months after stopping drug use. The next time you want to feel manic, remember that you also get to experience your depressive episodes.

Some complain that medications have taken take away their ambition and motivation. Many get accustomed or normalized to the energy levels and associated productivity while hypomanic. When this energy is taken away by medication, they say they don't feel normal. Their "normal" is really not normal for them; it's a product of their illness. Others report that their medications take the "edge" off their vitality and creativity. I have found that my creativity is still intact, although I had to go through an adjustment period to find a new way to express it. As far as my vitality after medication, I was able to work full-time with a higher degree of intellectual output than many without bipolar illness. Over a period of time, I realized that my vitality and creativity were hidden for a while, and they were still there for me to use later. I didn't lose them!

Others with the illness choose to live with hypomania and depressive symptoms without medication by managing their lives to minimize the effects on their moods. To keep their mood episodes from escalating, they learn to reduce environmental factors that aggravate their moods. Doing this takes much effort, and it may not be possible to do it and function fully in life. I prefer to adjust to medications and live without most of my symptoms of the illness.

Q-113. Is there any good to come out of the misery of having bipolar disorder?

One of the things that helped me live with bipolar illness is finding a purpose in it. I learned many important things about life and myself from having a "giant wrestling match" with this illness. Now, I have a certain degree of knowledge, wisdom, and insight that ordinary people don't have. I have firsthand knowledge about symptoms and how to cope with them that most doctors have to learn through books, schools, and observation. So what can I do with all my knowledge? I can choose to help others who are likewise afflicted with this illness. I can give away my experience, strength, and hope at bipolar support groups to those seeking it. When I help a suffering person in the midst of despair with the knowledge attained from the illness, I know that my pain and suffering with bipolar illness had great value. Using my experience acquired through years of this illness can help save another from the brink of suicide, and that makes all that I've been through valuable and worthwhile.

Can you learn something
out of having a bipolar disorder
that makes you more valuable in this life?

PR-9. A PSYCHIATRIST'S RESPONSE

Acceptance is basically a feeling state with thoughts about oneself and about one's life circumstances. Family, friends, the workplace, and the place one has in society are usually included in these thoughts. The letting go of the right and wrong of having a bipolar disorder is at the core of these thoughts and one's struggle for acceptance.

Early in any disastrous change in one's life, there is always denial or a refusal to accept what has happened to oneself. This is a normal reaction, but ultimately one must acknowledge the reality: "I have a bipolar disorder, and I must learn to live with it the best that I can." Acceptance is the absence of a continued struggle over this significant life change.

The struggle for acceptance within a patient is the domain of the therapist, and acceptance of one's reality should be a very high priority for the physician as well as the patient. The opposite of acceptance is defensiveness, which ranges from denial to rationalization and intellectualization, and none of these help engage (and resolve) the feelings associated with the illness.

Bipolar disorder doesn't include just the symptoms of mania, hypomania, or depression; it also includes the feelings and ideas the patient has about having the illness. Psychotherapy is the primary tool used to manage these feelings and ideas and is an important component in the treatment of individuals with bipolar disorder. The patient is profoundly affected by this very serious illness. Consequently, the patient needs support and encouragement, but above all, the wise therapeutic efforts of a psychiatrist who helps the patient deal realistically and honestly with his or her reality. "I have a bipolar disorder. What does that mean, and how shall I deal with it?" When a patient makes an honest and realistic effort to deal with his or her illness, the process of acceptance has begun.

LIVING WITH THE ILLNESS

**Q-114. I feel isolated and lonely, and I want to break out of this rut.
Do you have any thoughts on this?**

That we are social animals is clear and without question, and every person has the need to be known, loved, and accepted. We have a special problem in making friends because we have bipolar illness. We assume that almost everyone will reject us if they know about our illness. If our moods are not under sufficient control through medication, we don't feel up to the task of being a friend. So we give up or don't start the difficult search for meaningful relationships, and we take whatever "happens along." We tend to cut ourselves off from others and isolate ourselves. We have difficulty meeting new people and making new friends because *we think* that we're very different, not so much because of what others think. The role of friendships in the acceptance of our illness is very important and necessary if we are to move on in life. So I encourage you to begin working through the guidelines, listed below, that have helped me make new friends.

1. I must love and accept myself the way I am, realizing that my own improvement is a process.
2. If I want people to love me, I must give away love to others.
3. If I want to have a friend, I must be a friend.
4. I believe that my life was not meant to be alone and that true friends will be part of my life.
5. I recognize that it is in relationships that I was wounded and it is in

relationships that I will be healed. Therefore, I must form relationships.
6. I will identify the kind(s) of friend(s) whom I need and want.
7. I will not sit at home all day and night waiting for life to come to me.
8. I will discuss any reluctance to socialize with those I trust.
9. I must go where the kind of people I want are.
10. I will pursue friendships one day at a time with all the energy I have.
11. If I have anxiety and fear, I will work through them and not hide
    from them.
12. I will choose my friends wisely.
13. I will spend a regular amount of time reassessing my needs and plan-
    ning ways to fill them.
14. I accept that not everyone will like me and want to be my friend.
15. I will not give up, and I will not isolate or insulate myself from others.
16. I will not become co-dependent on another, and I realize that it is not
    my job to rescue all those who are in trouble.
17. I will end relationships that are not good for me.
18. I can say no to my friends.

Making quality friendships takes time.

**Q-115. I feel stuck within my circle of friends, and I want to be somebody
else. How can I change myself?**

You are implying that there is a deficit of your preferred attitudes, thoughts,
beliefs, personalities, and/or interests within your current circle of friends. Most
likely, this is a sign that you are growing and changing. Perhaps you are one of
the many people with bipolar disorder who socialize exclusively with other mentally ill people because you feel accepted and comfortable, and then sometime
later, you complain that your life isn't what you want. As you recover, your
needs in relationships change, and sometimes it may be hard to know where
you belong.

If you want to change, surround yourself with people whom you want to
become like. The truth is that we become like those we associate with whether
we want to or not. If you want to add something to your personality but don't
know how, you must place yourself around people who have your desired characteristics. If you want to become mentally healthy, be around mentally healthy
people. If you want to be a "winner," socialize with "winners." If you want a
positive attitude, be around positive people. If you want to give up old habits,
fill your life with people who have new desired habits. Initially, you may feel

that you don't fit in, and you'll have to "fake it" until you "make it" with that new group of friends. After some time you will begin to take on their attributes and thinking patterns and be changed as you desired.

Q-116. When I experience depressive symptoms, what do I tell people who say "just snap out of it," or "life's not that bad," or "just get over it"?

People tend to compare sadness with depression and tell you to "snap out of it." If they have never been depressed as we have, they are unable to identify with the intense feelings and torment felt. I think it is our responsibility to change our moods if possible, but no one is able to change deep depression of biological origins by willpower alone. If someone is constantly told to "snap out of it," they may never seek outside help because they are led to believe that they alone have the ability to end their depression. This results in a deadly trap where the person doesn't seek help.

These common statements made by family members are an example of what *not* to say to someone who is depressed. Comments like these are made by critical or ignorant people and make depressed people worse. Ignorant just means they haven't had a chance to become educated. Educated means they have learned some current information on capabilities, vulnerabilities, and symptoms of people with a mood disorder. More supportive comments based on education are the goal. The following statements are more *destructive* than productive for people with severe depression or bipolar illness:

Pull yourself up by the bootstraps.
It's for attention.
Life is what you make it.
Just don't think negative thoughts.
Think positive.
If I can do it, you can do it.
If you would just get involved with something with your time.
Quit being depressed.
Quit being lazy.
You are happy where you're at.
If you want to see something really bad, go to war.
You're intelligent, you're beautiful; how can you be depressed?
You are just escaping to the hospital.
Look at all you've got; how can you be depressed?
It will go away.
You don't know how bad things can be.

I used to walk 10 miles through the snow, and I never complained.

If you think things are bad now, you should have been around during the Great Depression.

If you love me, you wouldn't be depressed.

You don't want to face reality.

How can you hurt yourself?

Doesn't that hurt?

Have more control.

It is a beautiful day; go for a walk.

Here is one possible response to these statements: If my depression was due to a known cause such as a death in the family or a job loss, it would be my responsibility to change my moods in a reasonable period of time; however, I have bipolar disorder, a disorder that causes my moods to go up and down. Bipolar disorder is due to a biochemical imbalance in my brain that is out of my control. Depression is more than the blues; it includes extreme thinking distortions associated with that mood. I can't think my way out of biological depression even if I tried, and I have tried! Because the illness fluctuates and changes, you may falsely believe that my efforts caused a good month.

Your statements have oversimplified the solution and are grossly inappropriate. Do you really think that I would choose to feel horrible for so long? Don't you realize that if I could change it, I would! I have put a great deal of time, effort, and money into feeling better, and I am doing everything that I know to do to treat my illness. I suggest you learn more about bipolar disorder and its treatment, and I can give you the phone number for the National Depressive and Manic-Depressive Association. That organization has good reading material and can put you in contact with a support group for friends and families of people with bipolar disorder.

You can't judge others' insides by their outsides.

Q-117. How do I deal with the stigma of having bipolar disorder?

First, let me give you my definition of stigma. Stigma due to this illness is a feeling or sense of disgrace, dishonor, shame, or discredit with the impression of being blemished or stained in an ugly, undesirable way.

Stigma comes in the form of newspaper articles that misrepresent the truth and movies that make fun of the mentally ill. Nobody wants to be like the characters in the movies or newspapers. For the most part, everyone who is uneducated and unsympathetic to those with bipolar disorder instills a sense of stigma in us. Who takes stigma and puts it in us? We do! Why do we let that happen? We can't change what others think of us, but we don't have to accept and absorb their views of this illness as our own. I can change only the way I think about myself. I can choose to remove the stigma from myself and let the perpetrators keep it.

I will tell you what has helped me the most, and I don't mean to oversimplify it. The God I choose to believe in loves me and accepts me unconditionally, and I choose to believe what He says about me. If my God says that I am not disgraceful and not blemished and stained, shouldn't I choose to believe Him? Why should I believe others who want to put me down or label me? If my God says I'm OK, I can walk through life not caring what others think about me. And if God says I'm OK, I can love and accept myself without stigma.

Removing stigma takes time and effort.

Q-118. Is managing stress important?

Since many individuals with bipolar illness say that stress precipitates a period of depression or mania, I would say it is very important. Depending on the individual, significant stress for several weeks or months occurs prior to an episode. There are many contributing factors for stress in our lives and here are some: bipolar illness, job difficulties, inability to keep a needed relationship, lack of friends, problems with relatives, failure to reach a major goal, financial concerns, legal issues, other health issues, death of a friend or relative, sexual or sexuality issues, drug use, "dead-ends," and a heavy work or school load. The goal of all individuals with a bipolar disorder should be to minimize stress. We should make a complete list of all things in our life that cause stress, and good things can cause stress too. After deciding which issues we can do something about, we must purposely attempt to resolve them by removing stressful activities and relationships. We must make an effort for stress reduction because it doesn't happen by itself.

When you finally start to feel well due to the right medication(s), you may feel like going back to the same stress causing behavior in which you once engaged. This behavioral choice could cause a recurrence of partial symptoms. This is something to think about, isn't it?

Q-119. Are there any simple rules for managing my emotional health?

Pay close attention to the following on a daily basis.

1. Eat a proper diet.
2. Exercise.
3. Rephrase thoughts and achieve balanced thinking rather than negative, extreme, or catastrophic thinking.
4. Learn coping skills for the things that cause your moods to go up and down.
5. Seek stability rather than escalation.
6. Watch for negative self-esteem factors in your life and spread them out.
7. Use your pharmacist as a tool.
8. Use your doctor as a tool, and avoid the doctor-fix-me syndrome.
9. Learn the earliest signs of symptom escalation.
10. Make a conscious effort to improve your ability to stabilize your moods.

Another rule that has helped me greatly comes from Alcoholics Anonymous; it's called H.A.L.T. H stands for hungry, A for angry, L for lonely, and T for tired. When two or more of these four conditions exist, my emotional outlook stinks. Fortunately, I can do a lot to change these four conditions when I notice them beginning. The next time you feel your emotions "going to hell," think of the H.A.L.T. rule. Take action, and do your best to change the condition(s) that are affected. If you are hungry, eat. If you are angry, process your anger. If you are lonely, call somebody. If you are tired, rest.

Q-120. Do you set aside a certain amount of time daily just for yourself?

Yes, and I call that my quiet time. When I experienced periods of depression over a nine-and-a-half-year period, these quiet times became the most essential factor in surviving that period.

One of my quiet times was in the morning before I went to work. During this time, I established a closer conscious contact with God, which increased my faith enough to make it through the day. I started off the day with clear direction and a good attitude because my morning quiet time framed my outlook for the day. Before I had quiet times, I would start the day with whatever came to mind only to realize later that my day was disorganized and my attitude wasn't good.

After I got home from work in the late afternoon or early evening, I would have another quiet time. I would turn off the television or radio, and be all by myself. This was a time to make contact with God and clear my mind of the day's events. It was a time for reflection and a time to settle or resolve the day's conflicts. It was a time to assess the events in my day and do a reality check. This late quiet time got rid of any emotional baggage so that I didn't go to sleep with it.

The following are lists of activities that I do in two of my quiet times. If you don't like to call it a quiet time, make up a name that means something to you. Everyone has personal needs, and you can construct a quiet time of your own with a combination of activities that best suits you.

Early Morning Quiet Time (15 to 20 Minutes)

1. Listen to spiritual music that helps me get closer to God.
2. Sing my favorite uplifting, strengthening song(s).
3. Pray or talk to God about my concerns for the day.
4. Read spiritual material such as one day at a time readings, inspirational readings, or the Bible.
5. Meditate on what I have read and relate it to my life.
6. Dream and think about the good things I want for my future.

Late Afternoon Quiet Time (30 to 45 Minutes)

1. Pray or talk to God about today's events.
2. Read or listen to spiritual material.
3. Read or listen to other material that helps me with my mental health issues.
4. Meditate on what I have read and relate it to my life.
5. Spend some time planning, ordering, and scheduling the kind of life I want.
6. Write in a journal.

Q-121. Is patience needed in recovery?

For over nine long years, I waited and searched for relief from my depressive and hypomanic symptoms, and the hardest to endure was the deep depression. That kind of feeling was actually very painful and intense, and I endured it every day for up to several months at a time. Much of the time I didn't try to fight the depression because I knew it wouldn't do any good; I just waited passively for it to pass as someone would wait for a major physical injury to heal. Over time, I learned to tolerate great discomfort, and this kind of waiting while suffering taught me great patience. It was a lesson well learned because I needed patience to wait for what turned out to be years for an adequate treatment.

There were times in my recovery when I was either taught more patience or used the patience previously learned. Here are some of them: spending years misdiagnosed by a doctor, going through the trial and error approach of finding adequate medication, readjusting my relationships, learning new living skills, enduring the critical comments of everyone around me, rejection from my friends, and employment difficulties and the resulting financial burden.

In general, I would say that people who have been through years of bipolar illness are among the most patient that I have ever known. They have great courage, too!

Patience, you can't live without it.

Q-122. Several weeks ago I was diagnosed with bipolar disorder, and I am frightened to be trapped in my body with this illness. Did you feel this way too?

Having had symptoms for nine and a half years before being diagnosed, I was used to unexpected mood episodes. At many times, I felt as though I was under attack by some unnameable thing. I often asked myself questions like what are the dimensions of this thing that has attacked me? This problem seemed large and menacing, and at times I was frightened. I feared the illness because it was unpredictable, and I didn't understand it.

I knew that my mind was the tool used to think, but my mind wasn't working well. Did I have the mental capacity and ability left to find a solution to my bipolar symptoms? I wasn't sure, and I was scared. Everyone likes to be in control of their emotions and of their lives, but with bipolar disorder we're not; that in itself was frightening. I felt limited and confined much the way a runner would feel after breaking his leg. Both the runner and I still had to "move about" and function in life; we could manage although it was difficult, frustrating, and at times scary.

My illness became the dominating factor in my life through the years that I went undiagnosed and untreated. Once I was diagnosed and went through the medication process, my life became stable and the symptoms of the illness disappeared. All I had to do each day was take my pills, and that was very easy. With my mind not focused on bipolar illness anymore, I realized that the rest of my life was still there waiting for me to choose my next course of action; life was worth living. I heard a saying that helped me through this period, and it was "this too shall pass." Another variation was "all bad things will come to an end." These seemed reasonable, and I believed them. My fear faded away, and I soon discovered that I was neither hopeless nor helpless.

> Be ready to adapt
> because change is one thing
> that you can count on in life.

Q-123. Do the words I use in my speech and thoughts have an influence on my moods?

Yes. There is a whole area in psychology called cognitive therapy, and this therapy helps people to rephrase thoughts and achieve balanced thinking. I found that when words from outside of myself enter my mind, they become my thoughts. New feelings and moods are created when I react to these thoughts.

Here is an example. When I went through withdrawal from one medication, I described it to myself as a terrible, horrible experience. I actually believed that the experience was terrible and horrible, and my mood was one of great fear and dread. Anxiety and panic gripped me as though I were in a death struggle. Then I quickly changed the words I used, and said the experience was only unpleasant and moderately distressing. My reaction to those words gave a lower arousal and didn't result in a panic attack.

Have you ever wondered why you feel "down" sometimes? Maybe you are reacting to statements that you are telling yourself such as the following: Nobody likes me, I am no good, I'm ugly, I don't have a future, or I'll never be in love. If you say things like that over and over, how could you feel good? When you recognize this kind of a vicious thought process, stop it and question whether each of the statements is true. Then think up some accurate, truthful statements and start saying them over and over. Soon your mood will change for the better.

Have you ever been around an argument but not part of it? In a short period of time, the words associated with the argument enter your mind and are viewed as angry thoughts. Very quickly you will start to feel angry as your feelings are a reaction to your thoughts. If you want to get angry, listen to an angry conversation. If you want to be in a caring mood, listen to a caring conversation. If you want to change your mood, choose an appropriate conversation to listen to. Change your thoughts, and you'll change your mood.

I absorb positive statements.
I absorb courageous, reassuring statements.
I absorb calm, caring statements.
I absorb strong, capable, and optimistic statements.
I absorb the truth.

I reject negative statements.
I reject fearful statements.
I reject angry statements.
I reject helpless and hopeless statements.
I reject lies, half-truths, and exaggerations.

You are what you think.

Q-124. I have been unemployed for a while, and my self-esteem has been eroded. What can I do to improve my self-esteem?

Getting involved in some project or effort with others on a limited basis will help you. I recommend volunteer work because the benefits in regaining self-esteem can be enormous. Look for situations that require some effort on your part, that require you to use your experience and knowledge, that require you to interact with your peers, and that allow you to help others either directly or indirectly. After you have accomplished something that you set out to do as a volunteer, you will feel stronger and more self-confident. Volunteer work is great because you choose the organization, and you set the hours and length of involvement. When people notice that you have done a great job, they will praise you and ask you to do more. As you gradually increase your activities, your self-esteem will grow. Social skills, and perhaps new job skills, will grow and develop. And a nice part of volunteer work is that nobody has to know that you have a bipolar disorder; your life can be kept completely private.

Q-125. I'm having trouble making decisions. Is this normal for someone with bipolar disorder?

Some people with bipolar disorder have difficulty making decisions because they know that they don't have all the necessary information to make a choice. Others don't even know if they have all the facts, and they are lost in the process of decision making. A few are experiencing the side effects of changing medications when the decision making process is poor. Some are still experiencing the symptoms of the illness and don't feel well enough to make the right choice. Finally, indecision is not something familiar to only those with bipolar illness; many people have trouble making decisions regardless of whether they have this illness or not.

All of us want to know the outcome of our decisions before we make them, and for this reason many of us are afraid to make a mistake. All of us make one of these three choices at any given time whether we know it or not: (a) we make a decision and follow through with it, (b) we put off our decision to another specific point in time, or (c) we make no decision and take no action. Since we all have the ability to choose, we don't have to be paralyzed in the gray area of indecision and the associated emotions. There is a way to make a logical choice, and all you need is the courage to make a mistake.

I have outlined a decision making process below. We all go through this natural weighing process in our heads for smaller problems and decisions. This eight-step process is a logical one, and the process has much value when we have many musts, wants, and alternatives from which to choose. If you want to explore it in more depth, there are courses offered just for decision making and books written on the subject. Here are eight steps that have helped me to make complex decisions, and this process is best when you have several alternatives that are pretty close.

1. Define the decision that has to be made. Reduce all big decisions into smaller ones if possible.
2. Define all the things you "must" have as a result of your decision. These are called MUSTS.
3. Define all the things you "want" as a result of your decision. These are WANTS.
4. Rank all your WANTS and assign a relative numerical value to each. For example, the most important WANT gets a 10. If another WANT is only half as important to you as the "10," you give it a 5.
5. Generate alternatives to choose from in your decision making. Gather information relating to the alternatives by reading, researching, and asking questions. People are more likely to make better decisions once they know more facts regarding the alternatives. Example: If you are trying to decide which apartment complex to live in, go out and gather information on apartment complexes such as cost, size, availability, lease length, air conditioning, pool, gym room, etc. If you have only two apartment complexes in mind, you might want to search for more alternatives.
6. Take your list of MUSTS and go through your alternatives with it. If an alternative doesn't meet a MUST requirement, throw out that alternative.

7. With the remaining alternatives, compare each WANT with each alternative. How well does each alternative satisfy that particular WANT on a 1 to 10 point rating? Here is an example with three alternatives being compared numerically to three wants. Example: If ALT 2 gave you 90 percent of WANT 2, you would give it a 9 as is shown in the table below.

Example:

	From Step #4		Score from #7	
	Weight	ALT 1	ALT 2	ALT 3
WANT #1	10	5	7	3
WANT #2	5	6	9	1
WANT #3	2	2	4	8

Multiply the weight from Step #4 times the score from Step #7 and total them up for each alternative.

ALT 1 = 10(5) + 5(6) + 2(2) = 84
ALT 2 = 10(7) + 5(9) + 2(4) = 123
ALT 3 = 10(3) + 5(1) + 2(8) = 51

From these scores, Alternative 2 would be the best choice because it had the highest number; it would be your decision.

8. Assess the risks involved. Make a list of possible outcomes and consequences of your decision. When you accepted the risks involved, you are ready to act on your decision.

Don't forget to reach out to those you trust and admire for advice if you are having trouble making a decision.

Q-126. Changing medications scares me. What are my options?

Your fear comes from either not knowing what to expect in a medication change or from the memory of previous "bad" experiences. It's also possible that your fear may come from believing that you can't handle a medication change. In any event, all people who have used psychotropic medications have experienced some anxiety and fear at one point or another. You are not alone.

All medication changes will cause side effects in proportion to the rate of withdrawal or addition. If you must stop using a medication because it is causing dangerous side effects, your doctor will probably want it done quickly. Hospitalization may be needed because side effects due to rapid medication changes may be severely distressing. Sometimes, going off of a medication can bring back the symptoms of your illness, and your doctor might recommend that you be monitored in a hospital during that time.

If you don't have to change medications in a hurry, you could probably do it without going to a hospital. Depending on your sensitivity level, you could decrease/add your old/new medication by the smallest increment that is available every other day. Your side effects will be lower because withdrawal/addition will be slower; however, your illness could come back and stay longer because you are taking more time changing medications. Depending on the severity of your bipolar symptoms, you could still have to be hospitalized. I recommend discussing your concerns and your options with your doctor, and both of you can come up with a suitable plan for changing medications.

There is a way to change medications and not be scared!

Q-127. I just was diagnosed with a bipolar disorder. I'm also a recovering drug addict and attend Narcotics Anonymous. How do I overcome my strong convictions not to use any drugs, even prescription drugs, in the treatment of my illness?

I understand that you are in a dilemma over what course of action to take, and most people in your situation experience a similar depth of concern and confusion. I assume that you have spent a great deal of time and effort self-medicating your ups and downs with "street" drugs before you entered your program. Throughout your recovery process, the idea that drugs of all types are inappropriate in treating your ups and downs was ingrained within you. You probably think that the use of any type of drug now is equivalent to failure or relapse in your Narcotics Anonymous program. I also assume that your goal in life now is to get your spiritual, emotional, and physical life into good health without the use of drugs.

But which drugs? The drugs used to treat bipolar disorder won't get you high and they're not addictive. They'll just stop your moods from going up and down due to your illness and make you feel normal. The idea of medicating your ups and downs isn't new to you; in the past, you just used the wrong drugs. You used dangerous addictive drugs to do that because you didn't know

how to treat your illness. Now that you know the cause of your mood disturbances is biological in origin, can you see that there is nothing wrong with
treating that medical problem appropriately? No amount of 12-Step work is going to fix a problem of biochemical origins. The ups and downs you have due
to bipolar illness will not be cured by a recovery program for the disease of
addiction.

I recommend that you try a support group for recovering drug addicts who
have a dual diagnosis of mental illness. Call your county mental health association for a meeting location. I'm sure you'll be able to fully discuss your concerns over medications at those meetings and eventually find "the courage to
change the things you can." With medications, you won't be a failure; you'll
be a winner.

First things first.

Q-128. I can't get to sleep at night. What can I do?

At times, everybody has trouble falling asleep, and there are many possible
reasons for this. For most with bipolar disorder, a poor night's sleep may signal
the beginning of a mood episode. Some have had a stressful day and feel "wound
up," and they haven't given themselves time to unwind before going to bed.
Others have intense stimuli entering their minds in the hour or two preceding
bedtime when they should be listening, watching, or engaging in calming events
rather than exciting ones. Also, late-night conversations with others may give
too much stimulus; lying in bed and reading a book or listening to a relaxation
tape would be more beneficial. Coffee drinkers absorb caffeine late in the day
and wonder why they can't get drowsy. If you just jump into bed after going
90 miles an hour all day, you cannot expect to fall asleep right away! Think
honestly about the effects of your activities on your ability to fall asleep. The
important thing to remember is to prepare yourself for a night's sleep if you
had a bad day.

Sometimes I had a fear of not falling asleep because I remembered how I
felt after five hours of sleep when my normal was eight and one-half hours.
With little sleep, the next day was always miserable. I used to roll around in
bed watching the minutes and hours tick off, and that contributed to anxiety.
My fear and anxiety kept me from sleeping so I had to believe that there was
no danger to missing a few hours sleep.

I have heard it said that if I can't fall asleep, I should read a book or watch
TV. I disagree with that because I would only be working my brain rather than

resting it. I have a better way that involves fooling my brain into thinking I am asleep, and I do that by eliminating all stimuli. The steps are as follows:

1. Go to bed at your normal time or as close to it as possible.
2. Hide the clock so that you can't see it.
3. Turn out all lights and anything that's making noise.
4. Get in your most favorite relaxed position in bed.
5. Lie there without moving a muscle because muscle movement will provide stimuli to the brain.
6. Think about anything you wish, but make them calm, reassuring, positive thoughts.

After doing these six steps, the stimuli to the brain have been reduced considerably. After an hour or so of motionlessness, you'll discover that you have dreamed, and that you had been sleeping some. This method works every time for me. Although only slightly tired the next day, I'm able to function and do all that is required of me.

If you still need more help in falling asleep, some medications have a drowsiness side effect that may aid you in falling asleep. You could explore varying your medications accordingly with your doctor. Discuss your sleep problems with your doctor, and don't hesitate to talk to a sleep expert if your doctor's advice doesn't help.

Q-129. On weekends I like to stay out several hours past my normal bedtime, but the next day I always feel bad. Can anything be done to help this situation?

I have heard similar stories from people who work different shift schedules in the same week. Most people without bipolar illness also have some sort of symptoms the next day following a "late-nighter." When I stay up several hours past my normal bedtime, the next day I feel shaky, nervous, irritable, somewhat emotional, sedated, mentally sluggish, and sometimes have mild to moderate short-term bipolar symptoms typical for my illness. I believe that I'm more sensitive to changes in sleep patterns than most people, and many people with bipolar illness have told me that they have a similar sensitivity.

Because a regular sleep pattern is essential for predictable mood stability, you might want to revise or establish your own schedule that suits some of your late-night needs yet doesn't cause sleep-related aftereffects. For each of the seven days of the week, try getting up in the morning at the same time and going to sleep at night at the same time. Also, do the more stimulating activities earlier in the evening to keep them from charging up your mind right before bedtime.

Listen to what your body is telling you!

Q-130. I have just begun taking medication for my bipolar disorder. Is my diet important?

You should research the medications that you are on and see what is said about weight gain side effects. Some drugs stimulate the appetite, and some don't. For the same drug, some people can have an excessive weight gain while others have very little. People who are overweight prior to drug therapy tend to gain the most weight. From the beginning of taking medications that have a potential for a weight gain side effect, you should construct a sensible diet and watch the calories if you wish to maintain your same weight. If your medications make you thirsty, don't consume a lot of high-calorie drinks. Moderate exercise is also essential in keeping the pounds off because it burns calories and reduces the appetite. Your doctor can help you determine an adequate diet plan if you have the potential to gain unwanted weight.

Whether your medication has a weight gain side effect or not, proper nutrition in recovery is necessary. If you want to repair your body (the brain is part of the body) and get it working at peak performance, you must give yourself all the right building blocks including a balanced diet low in fat and sugar. Make sure you are drinking a sufficient amount of water (most people don't). You might want to take vitamins, but don't overdo it.

When I started taking lithium carbonate, I gained a pound every two weeks for a year. I kept eating the same way that I did prior to lithium; my metabolism slowed down, and I gained weight. I was slender to begin with, and I didn't mind the first ten pounds. My weight continued to creep up, and I didn't have much willpower to go on a diet. I wish I had reduced my calorie intake and watched my weight during this period because getting five or ten pounds off today is very difficult.

Q-131. Could food additives cause strange psychological phenomena?

Yes. I'll give you an example from my life. When I first started dieting, I ate many things that contained Nutrasweet. After several days, I developed the worst headache that I ever had, and I couldn't even move without severe head pain. I was nauseated, and I vomited several times. I felt strange, and a feeling of unreality was present; I thought I was losing my mind. I immediately stopped eating and drinking anything that contained Nutrasweet. The following day all my symptoms were gone. Later, I doubted that Nutrasweet caused the symptoms because I believed the government wouldn't allow that on the market if it caused people such illness. But I was wrong! Several days passed, and I decided to drink two diet soft drinks containing Nutrasweet in the same day. The following day, the same bad side effects were present. Several more months passed, and I drank just one can of diet soda containing Nutrasweet. It happened again, and I felt terrible. After those experiences, I have made sure that Nutrasweet isn't present in anything that I eat or drink, and I ask restaurants if they use Nutrasweet in anything too. I asked around to see if Nutrasweet bothered anybody else. My sister had the same reactions to it as I did, but the rest of my family didn't. I discovered one friend who had the exact same negative reactions, and I've even seen this issue discussed on TV!

The point to all of this discussion is to advise you to check the chemical additives in the food and drink you consume. Everything you consume may be legal, but it could still make you sick. Additives may cause moderate to severe symptoms that are similar to a psychiatric disorder. If you are not sure about specific chemicals such as saccharin, monosodium glutamate, preservatives, and those in "brain-smart" drinks that "expand your mind," or anything else unfamiliar, ask your doctor if the additive can cause a negative reaction in you. Also, ask your pharmacist and/or the manufacturer(s) of your medication whether the additive has the potential to cause negative side effects. If you consume an unfamiliar additive for the first time, do so in a low dosage and check for side effects.

Q-132. Can exercise help?

I don't believe that exercise can prevent or restrain major episodes of depression or mania. Based on my own experience, extensive physical workouts do not prevent these mood disturbances; however, mild exercise may relieve stress and tension, and this reduction usually helps minor depressive symptoms.

Exercise is a necessity for everyone to be physically healthy, not just people with bipolar illness. I have found exercise to be very valuable because of its contribution to the following areas: weight control, stress reduction, muscle tone and strength, overall healthier feeling, better sleep, and more endurance. What someone can do with exercise varies with the individual. I know a few who exercise a great deal, and in the most extreme example, one even ran a marathon while on lithium. Most of the people with bipolar illness with whom I have talked report that their level of physical output had permanently decreased once their illness had begun and medication started. So don't compare yourself to your past physical accomplishments. My entire exercise routine consists of walking 30 to 50 minutes a day on the beach. I get a suntan, watch people, and have time to think; I really look forward to my walks. Finally, here are a few suggestions for your new exercise routine.

1. Try to do any exercise routine that you choose, but listen to your body's response and don't overdo it. Do something you enjoy.
2. Let your doctor know what you plan to do. If you are on lithium, sweating too much will raise your lithium level. Other medications should be checked to see if they are adversely affected by your exercise routine.
3. Set new realistic goals.
4. Find a friend with whom to exercise and make it a social outing.

Q-133. Will my sexual energy diminish once I begin medications?

People who are manic or hypomanic tend to have increased sexual energy and activity, and this excess will be reduced when you take medication because your manic episodes will disappear (hopefully). Those who are experiencing depression may have their sexual desire increased to a normal level once medications begin. And don't be surprised if you see a decrease in your normal-mood sexual energy when you compare it to your pre-illness days 5, 10, or 20 years ago because most people experience a decrease over time.

Some people with bipolar illness report that their sexual desires are slightly reduced after they have been on a particular medication. I have even heard that some men who are taking certain antidepressants are not able to get an erection. So, I recommend that you research your medication(s), and see if lowered sexual desires or performance problems are possible side effects.

Q-134. I've been unemployed for nine months, and my mind has turned to "jello." What can I do about it?

You probably have heard the saying, "If you don't use it, you'll lose it." It's true. Keeping the mind active is very important, or you will lose your edge and become mentally sluggish. You can sharpen your mind by choosing one of the following.

1. Read a self-help book or one that enhances your education or career goals. Study a particular textbook that interests you and work through any example problems.
2. Socialize with others and have meaningful intellectual discussions.
3. Pursue your hobbies in-depth.
4. Do volunteer work.
5. Take a class or school course.
6. Work part-time.

Regaining your sharp edge may be a slow process at first, and you may resist it. In my most recent experience, I chose to study a career-related subject using a textbook. At first, I attempted to study one-half hour per day, but I frequently read a page without remembering a thing. My mind drifted while reading, and I started thinking about something else. Focus came only with practice. After two months of patient effort, I studied up to four hours a day and remembered almost everything. My mind then was back up to speed, and it didn't feel like jello anymore.

Think of your mind as a muscle. Exercise it!

Q-135. Did you ever feel the need to develop better social skills?

Yes. When I got into my 20's, I discovered that my social skills were inadequate for the things I wanted to do. I chose these skills from the limited pool my family, friends, and peers provided. Coming from a dysfunctional family, my skills were the ones I used to cope with the environment as I grew up, and these coping skills were not necessarily good social skills in the present.

After my bipolar illness began at age 20, I began to withdraw from what I would call a normal life; I retreated to a safe and comfortable way of life. Over a period of years, my social skills weakened and deteriorated from lack of use. As I started to recover from everything that happened to me in life including bipolar illness, I wanted to reconnect to people. I found this process to be quite frustrating and awkward.

I wanted to know how to make friends and how to keep them. Learning how to get along with difficult people who were sometimes irritable, out of control, angry, and strong-willed was necessary. I wanted to feel comfortable interacting with strangers in a social setting. Communicating more effectively with relatives, friends, co-workers, supervisors, my doctors, people at support groups, and people at church became important.

Social skills are needed to achieve the kind of life many of us dream about. Here are some helpful activities where this learning process can begin.

1. Seek out people who have the social skills you admire and learn by their example. Develop friendships with these people.
2. Be around people in different social settings.
3. Read books on social skills, effective communication, and social etiquette.
4. Find someone to be your mentor for social skills development.
5. Be willing to risk making a mistake.
6. Find people who will give you honest feedback about your social skills and progress.
7. Treat others as you would want to be treated.

At a time in the past, I found myself out of a job, lacking in meaningful relationships, and filled with apprehension over restarting my social life. When I was making phone calls in an attempt to find a starting place for socializing, I was told about an organization called The Meeting Place, Inc. near downtown San Diego, California. I discovered that The Meeting Place, Inc., was a client-run drop-in center or clubhouse for those with mental or emotional disorders financed by grants and private donations. Furthermore, they were open five days a week (Wednesday through Sunday) and offered self-help groups, art classes, and a place to sit down and have a conversation with someone who has a similar background. I continue to go to this place several times a week, and I usually stay anywhere from ten minutes to two hours. I participate in some of their activities and leave when I choose. This group helped me get used to people again. If you want to begin enhancing your socialization process, I suggest that you call your county's mental health association and see if a similar group is near you.

Q-136. I feel that I am not doing what I really want to do with my life. How did you better determine your career path?

About 10 months after I went on disability, I started to wonder about what career I wanted in the future. I knew that there were some things that I really enjoyed, and these elements were missing from my most recent job. Also, I felt different than many of my co-workers as though we weren't completely in the same sphere of interests.

I got a course catalog from a university extension, and I looked through it. One of the courses was on career and vocational assessment, and it cost around $200 for the three 3-hour classes. In the classroom, I took several standard tests as follows: Strong Interest Inventory, Holland's Self-Directed Search, Myers-Briggs Type Indicator, and a career values assessment.

A clearer view as to why my full-time job in engineering had been less than satisfactory emerged. The tests showed that I have an equal interest in technical and social aspects. My engineering job dealt primarily with technical information, and the social aspects were seldom used. If I could blend these together in a future career or work some in both fields, I would be much happier. The results of this course confirmed what I had felt but hadn't been able to put into words. Over the past fifteen years that I have had bipolar illness, a new and important interest in social areas had resulted. Instead of engineering only with steel and concrete, I developed and added an interest in engineering people's thoughts, dreams, attitudes, and behavior.

I recommend taking a course such as the one I took if you want to reevaluate your career path or just want to find yourself. Check with a university extension or a community college for a similar course. Your doctor also should be able to tell you where to take these tests, and your doctor may even give them. The psychology department at a local college or university may provide these tests at a much cheaper cost but without the valuable explanations given in a classroom.

A new you may be waiting to be discovered.

Q-137. I can't afford living by myself now that I am on disability. How can I find a new place to live knowing that I have a bipolar disorder?

In addition to the financial burden of finding treatment for a bipolar disorder, many must find adequate housing with already strained budgets and have little choice whether to have a roommate or not. We should have compassion for those who are in a struggle to find what most people take for granted, a place to live.

Most people value their independence, and they like to come and go from their home without making compromises with fellow occupants. If disability or low income will not allow you to live by yourself in a house or apartment, you may have to consider either a roommate or a smaller place to live. Others are tired of living alone, and they may want to have roommates such as yourself for companionship. If you are considering a roommate situation, consider the following questions:

1. Will you have control over your living space?
2. Can you get privacy when you want it?

3. Will you have spiritual and moral compatibility with your roommate(s)?
4. Can you count on everyone to pay their share of the bills? If they don't, will you have to pay more?
5. Does the situation meet your standards for quietness?
6. Is there openness between all roommate(s) about illnesses?
7. Does the other roommate work?
8. If a roommate is home all day with you, will that be acceptable?
9. Does it matter whether roommates are male or female?
10. Is the location of the residence acceptable?
11. Can you store all your belongings there?
12. Is the phone readily available for your use?
13. Are there any limitations and are these acceptable?
14. Are the "house rules" known and acceptable?
15. If you get depressed or manic, will your roommates know how to respond effectively?
16. If a roommate works at night and sleeps all day, can you live with that?
17. If you don't like the place and arrangements, can you move out without penalty?
18. Are the neighbors quiet?
19. Do you want to live with others who have a mental illness or with those who are sympathetic to the mentally ill?
20. Will you have your own bedroom and bathroom?
21. Will a roommate have to provide you with transportation?
22. How well do you know your roommate?
23. Can you get along with your roommate?

If you want more than one or two roommates, you might want to consider a group home with room and board provided, or a more supervised residential care facility depending on your needs. Also, numerous single room occupancy units are available in motels, lodges, and inns at reduced weekly or monthly rates. For these options, you could contact your local branch of the National Alliance for the Mentally Ill for lists of places where you might stay. Also, call your local mental health association and ask for their assistance, referral, and recommendation. Has anybody thought of making a roommate bulletin board for mental health clients?

PR-10. A PSYCHIATRIST'S RESPONSE

Thirty years of practicing medicine has convinced me of a basic truism: Man cannot live alone. Living with the illness truly means living with the illness *with others*. We need one another. We cannot live any kind of decent, meaningful life unless we have friends and people who care deeply about us.

Patients with bipolar disorder have special needs for friends and family who care enough about their bipolar family member to learn about the illness, to understand how it has specifically effected their loved ones, and how he or she is responding to it. The patient cannot live a quality life, with or without bipolar disorder, if he or she does not have friends or family members who reach out, make an effort, overcome disturbed and troubled behavior, stand beside the person, and walk with him or her through the very difficult times that he or she will endure. The very best psychotherapy cannot take the place of caring family and friends.

The doctor is not likely to be there for patients when they are in the depths of despair, in the middle of the night, unable to sleep, and dealing with "terrors of the night." The doctor and the medications can modify the patient's behaviors, attitudes, and ways of understanding the disorder, but they cannot take the place of caring, concerned, and loving family and friends.

The family may be there, but the patient must make an effort to reach out and form a new relationship with each family member. The family member is not going to understand how the patient feels unless the patient describes his or her feelings, is vulnerable, open, and willing to put all of his or her cards on the table, risking rejection and indifference. We all find this difficult, but particularly difficult for those struggling with the symptoms of bipolar disorder. Members of support groups find it much easier to understand and empathize with the patient because they have experienced the same or similar symptoms. They can reach out, empathize, comfort, and support the patient in ways that family and friends may find difficult or even impossible.

In my professional opinion, stress is one of the most important factors in a person's life. I believe that stress plays a very important role in precipitating hypomanic, manic, or depressive episodes. Bipolar patients do better when they reduce their stress significantly.

We all live in a fast-paced environment with news of the world constantly bombarding us with stories of atrocities, famine, and other horrifying situations. As human beings, we respond to these stories and these portrayals of human despair and tragedy. This is stress. Stress not only comes from our family members who drink excessively, gamble, drive recklessly, have divorced or are in a dysfunctional marriage, or may have a hot explosive temper. Stress also comes from being aware of all the difficulties that we experience as a nation, as a community, and even as a world. Global warming can be a source of stress for people. The possibilities of earthquakes here in southern California is very stressful for many, and driving on a freeway is extraordinarily stressful for others. So many of these stressors cannot be avoided.

The bipolar patient has added stressors that derive from the illness itself. He or she must find a physician, perhaps even a hospital to help. Money must be found to buy the medicine and pay the doctor. The patient must deal with the consequences of his or her bipolar disorder behaviors, such as spending foolishly, excessive drinking, and getting a ticket for driving under the influence. As an example, I recall that one patient bought a very expensive cat when she and her husband were desperately trying to make ends meet. Dealing with the consequences of these behaviors is very stressful and perpetuates and exacerbates the illness.

Family, friends, the patient's doctor, and the patient must make every effort to reduce the stressors in the patient's life. I believe this is absolutely essential for the recovery and the maintenance of good health with the bipolar patient. Reducing stress does not mean that you have to move into a convent or a monastery, and it doesn't mean that you must move to the mountains or to a desert island. Reducing stress does mean turning off the radio and television set more often or turning the volume down very low. Avoiding tense and provoking situations whenever possible is another necessity. You must avoid the old crowd who enjoyed the hypomanic behaviors that egged you on in your drinking, drug use, or other many varied manic behaviors. These kinds of stressors can and must be avoided for the patient to recover from his or her illness and achieve mood stability.

SUPPORT GROUPS

Q-138. Where is a good place to find out current information about bipolar disorders?

Support meetings are valuable places to get the most current information on this illness if they have an educational or lecture part to the meeting led by a medical professional. Our doctors may be excellent sources of information assuming they put out the effort to keep up with all the latest on bipolar illness and its treatment. Although books may be great places to find out about this illness, meetings have people with real illnesses that you can see firsthand. Support groups have helped me to see my illness in the context of many others' illnesses. I know how my illness "fits" within the broad range of symptoms of this illness, and I have a clearer idea of the spectrum of mania and depression.

Q-139. Whom can I contact to find the location of support groups?

1. Your county mental health association should have quite an extensive list of support groups in your area. Check your phone book for the number.

2. National Depressive and Manic-Depressive Association
   730 North Franklin Street, Suite 501
   Chicago, IL 60610
   Phone (312) 642-0049; FAX (312) 642-7243
   Contact them for local NDMDA groups.

111

3. National Alliance for the Mentally Ill
   2101 Wilson Boulevard, Suite 302
   Arlington, VA 22201
   Phone (703) 524-7600; FAX (703) 524-9094
   Contact them for local NAMI groups.

4. Ask other people you know with this illness.

5. Ask your doctor.

Q-140. What is the purpose of a support group?

The purpose is to provide the opportunity to share our experience, knowledge, strength, hope, and caring as it relates to our illness and obtain feedback. We can identify with other people and reconnect to the human species in a support group. The goal of a group is to increase self-understanding, to improve our confidence, self-esteem, and self-acceptance.

The group, however, should not pretend to replace the advice of a physician, but the group will improve the patient-physician relationship by providing information and support to the person with bipolar illness. If you have any questions regarding the opinions, advice, and facts presented by a support group, discuss them with your doctor.

Q-141. How is a support group structured?

Typically, a support group is for friends, families, and individuals living with bipolar disorder. Meetings may have two parts with the first hour as an educational meeting, led by a medical professional, which includes everyone. The second hour may have a separate meeting for individuals with the illness and another meeting for friends and family. Sometimes there may be no educational meeting, and other variations in this approach or meeting structure exist.

Usually, time is available for an individual to share needs and concerns and get feedback. The group may go "around the circle" giving every member an opportunity to share briefly. Or, people with an urgent need to share may be given first priority at the beginning of the meeting and take more than a few minutes each. In the latter situation, many will be unable to share in a large group. In any case, some members stay after meetings and like to talk informally.

Q-142. What do I say in a support group?

Everyone in a group is an "expert" on their own life's story with their illness. Sometimes they think they have a monopoly on the overall truth about this disorder. So when talking, be yourself, and give *your own experience*; no one should argue with that. Some people resent being told what to do, and giving your own experience avoids telling others what to do. Avoid preaching and talking down to others. Rather, be uplifting and remember that many in a group have low self-esteem and need positive things said about them. Put yourself in their shoes, and treat them the way you want to be treated. Be slow to speak, and think before you speak. Avoid running on and on without letting any one in the group have a word; dialogue helps us, not monologue. If someone "runs on" for more than a few minutes, interrupt him or her in an attempt to get a two-way conversation going. If the person doesn't take the hint that others need to speak, stop the individual and let him or her know that others need to participate in the discussion. Trying to keep one person from dominating the group can be awkward, but correcting the problem happens so fast that it shouldn't interrupt the spirit of the group.

Q-143. What statements, rules, or guidelines does your support group have?

Here are some general guidelines that my group adopted.

1. If we have more than 8 to 12 people, we will divide into two or more groups. One will be a larger group that is more structured and interactive than the smaller group.
2. In all our discussions, keep in mind that our purpose is to provide the opportunity for each individual to share his or her own experience, knowledge, strength, hope, and caring.
3. Everyone's responsibility is to manage the group and keep it under control.
4. The meeting is not a platform for expressing outside views unless they directly relate to your struggles with bipolar disorder. The meeting isn't a platform for expressing moral views, judgment, condemnation, or political views.
5. Some of us don't like to be interrupted when speaking. If you feel this way, please state this at the beginning of your time to speak; however, if your conversation is irrelevant to bipolar issues, you will be interrupted and asked to make it relevant.
6. The group isn't a place where one person dominates the meeting by talking incessantly. If you talk too much, you will be asked to give others a chance to speak. We should be more willing to listen than to talk.

7. Some of us do not like to be asked a lot of questions. Don't ask questions needlessly.
8. The group isn't a place where members diagnose each other with this illness or play the role of a therapist. The group isn't a place where members play pharmacist and tell you what medications and dosages are right for you. The group doesn't take the place of psychotherapy or counseling by a professional.
9. Avoid making statements with the word "you" in them. Instead, use the word "I." Let your statements reflect your personal experience, not someone else's experience or a theoretical experience.
10. Do not give advice unless requested. Instead, giving our experience is more desirable.
11. New statements, guidelines, and rules must be agreed upon by at least two-thirds of the group members present.

Now that you have read these eleven general guidelines, I'm sure you can see the types of group problems we tried to prevent. You probably will have to adopt similar guidelines in your group.

Q-144. Do people get out of control at meetings?

Quite often someone will have an irritable mood or other symptoms of the illness while at a meeting. Very infrequently, some of these people get overly angry, argumentative, and hostile to the point of seriously disrupting a meeting. Hopefully the group, particularly the leaders, will handle this in an appropriate manner. Normally more than one individual escorts the "disrupter" outside where they will discuss the situation, evaluate what is really going on, diffuse the situation, and help the individual. In some cases, one or more persons may be manic and psychotic, and no amount of talking to them will help. If they are a danger to themselves or others, they may be taken to a hospital emergency room. The building's security personnel may have to be called to remove them from the building and, in rare cases, the police may be asked to take over the situation. To repeat, people at meetings rarely get out of control, and if the group is being run well, disruptive people will be dealt with quickly and compassionately before it gets out of hand.

Q-145. What if I don't like the group?

If you don't like your first meeting, remember that every time that group meets it is unique. The next meeting will be different, and it may be what you have been seeking. Many support groups recommend that you go to a group three to six times before deciding to stay or leave the group; however, I've been to support groups and have known immediately whether they were good for me or not. Remember too, that these groups are made of people like yourself and that they are not perfect. My advice is go to a few more meetings if you think the group is on the borderline of being acceptable. If the group is obviously not for you, don't go again. But don't give up your search because better groups do exist. Only you can be the judge if a group is good for you, and I'm sure there is one out there that will meet your needs.

Q-146. Are there other types of meetings that might be of help to people with bipolar illness?

Yes. After medications removed most of my bipolar symptoms, I was still quite capable of feeling the normal range of emotions brought about by my reactions to the outer environment. I wanted to improve the way I responded and interacted with people, and I needed a method to deal with nervous symptoms and sensations that I didn't understand. One of these self-help groups, called Recovery, Inc., helped me manage my thoughts and beliefs that affected emotions such as anger, fear, panic, and anxiety. Recovery, Inc., is a nonprofit foundation that sponsors free self-help groups using a structure of principles developed by the late psychiatrist, Dr. Abraham Low.

Laypersons (like myself) learn and practice applying these principles to the frequent, trivial frustrations of everyday life to counteract and avoid chronic anxiety, depression, anger, panics, compulsions, phobias, and other nervous symptoms. Emphasis is upon early identification of the symptoms of emotional upset and the recognition that symptoms are distressing but not dangerous. Recovery, Inc., shows that symptoms can be endured rather than allowed to affect behavior and to induce the vicious cycle including feelings of danger which aggravate the symptoms.

Members do not diagnose, counsel, treat, or advise one another, and they are expected to follow the authority of their own physician. Members learn from each other how to use Recovery principles in their daily lives to control behavior and to reevaluate and adopt more realistic thoughts, beliefs, and attitudes.

You can find out where Recovery, Inc., meets by calling or writing them at the following address.

Recovery, Inc.
802 North Dearborn Street
Chicago, IL 60610
Phone (312) 337-5661; FAX (312) 337-5756

Other helpful groups exist, and your local mental health association would usually have listings for some of the groups below.

1. Mental health clients seeking employment help, or a networking group for unemployed professionals.
2. Families of the mentally ill.
3. Advocacy group of families, friends, consumers, and professionals dedicated to the care, treatment, and rehabilitation of persons with mental illness.
4. Those with a dual diagnosis of alcoholism or drug addiction combined with mental illness.
5. Those of certain age ranges.
6. Ethnic groups.

PR-11. A PSYCHIATRIST'S RESPONSE

In my experience, support groups have been vital in helping my patients make good use of their therapy and medication, and groups are very helpful to those who are having difficulty handling their lives. I have never had a bad experience with my patients going to a support group, and these groups have never interfered with my efforts in helping my patients. I am sure that there have been times when a support group has not been helpful, but I have never found one to be harmful or destructive to any of my patients.

Many of my patients, however, especially those who are introverted and reluctant to meet new people, initially have a difficult time entering and engaging in a support group. I encourage and push hard for my patients to risk the uncomfortable feelings of being a new member. For them I suggest that they try a meeting, and I remind them that their initial discomfort will change to comfort. I remind them that every member of the group has been a new member, and the vast majority of them understand what it feels like to be a new member. Most groups are very gentle, supportive, and kind to new members. They may ask a few general questions about you as a new member, but they will neither expect you to participate much nor expect you to be open, vulnerable, or forthcoming. Especially, they will understand that there will be times when you don't feel well. They will expect that the first session or two will be difficult for you and will make allowances and will be understanding of your discomfort. Overall, you alone decide your level of involvement and participation with a group.

I think you will find that joining a support group will be one of the most useful experiences you will have in recovering from your bipolar disorder. You will gain the support, understanding, knowledge of the illness, and acceptance that you will get nowhere else but from a support group. As a physician, I know what I can do, and what I cannot do. I cannot do what a support group can do. I can be a good psychiatrist, but I cannot take the place of a support group. Therefore, I urge you to search for a support group that meets your needs. It may not be the first bipolar disorder group that you attend. It may even be another form of mental health recovery group, even a 12-step group but, if you keep looking, you will find one that will meet your needs and will be a tremendous source of help to you in dealing with your illness.

FAMILY AND FRIENDS

Q-147. Does the family of someone with bipolar illness need support from others?

Yes. When the illness starts, there is usually great confusion in the family. Usually this occurs over what has happened to their family member. The rest of the family may take varying viewpoints that tend to divide the family's effort to help the person with the illness. Some want to distance themselves from the person with the illness to avoid accepting the reality of mental illness so close to themselves. When they find out there is a genetic component, they have a fear that they are going to get the illness too. Others view having this illness as a kind of moral weakness akin to having "mental leprosy"; they do not want to publicly or privately admit it is in their family. Some pretend that nothing has changed, and they refuse to acknowledge that the family member has an illness; denial is their way of coping. Others don't want to be around to see the damage created and experience the associated pain and disappointment; maybe they believe "out of sight, out of mind." And a heroic few dive right in to minimize the damage done during a manic episode and get the person the help they need.

Families tend to be devastated when they first hear that a close relative has bipolar illness, and shame and guilt are probably the two most common reactions. Because families are reluctant to talk about these things, they may try to resolve it without going outside of the family; they'll find few answers that way. Family members need support and discussion, and they need outside help to work through it.

Because many in the family may have little idea what has happened to their family member, I strongly recommend that they learn all they can about the illness. Secondly, they should participate in support group meetings for families of the mentally ill and/or for families with bipolar illness in them. Family members then can start talking about their thoughts and feelings in a safe and supportive environment. Soon, communication within the family will improve, and perhaps the family will be strengthened from having this illness in a family member.

I suggest reading some books specifically for families and friends found in the NDMDA Bookstore Catalog (Phone 312-642-0049; FAX 312-642-7243).

Q-148. When a parent has bipolar illness, doesn't that destabilize the whole family?

In most cases, yes. When I grew up, I knew three brothers whose mother was mentally ill. Most of the time, I saw the mother as a stable, gentle, lovable person, and this was the person I knew as their mother.

On a few occasions, I saw her when she wasn't her usual self. The sound of her voice had changed, and she argued with her family, which was not characteristic of her. She lost a lot of weight and looked better than before. She spontaneously mentioned the names of cities and states for no reason, and nobody knew what she was talking about. One time, she took money out of her savings, went to a car dealer, and paid the sticker price for a new car. This didn't seem too unreasonable until I found out that she didn't know how to drive. Shortly afterwards, she packed her things and moved to Ohio from North Carolina. In Ohio, she bought or rented a house. Why Ohio? Nobody knew. One of the three brothers went with her, and all his friendships and school activities were cut short. Some time later, her normal self returned, and she moved back home to North Carolina; she always eventually came back to her normal self.

Imagine the frustration and heavy concern on the part of her family for her well being. Imagine the confusion and fear in the family when their mother became someone else unidentifiable and unpredictable. Their fear increased in proportion to the change viewed in their mother. The family had only a few friends in the neighborhood; they were isolated, and most of the neighbors kept their distance as if the family had a contagious disease. With all the family's time and energy going into dealing with a mental disorder, they didn't keep up their house as the rest of the neighborhood did. Their yard was often not mowed, and the house looked old with faded paint and partial paint jobs. Storage boxes and assorted items littered the front porch and many places inside their house. And finally, they were disillusioned with the medical community over the decades of their doctors' efforts in trying unsuccessfully to help the mother. The family was shy and withdrawn from much social life, but they were very understanding and believed in each other; they never gave up.

After decades of misdiagnosis as a paranoid schizophrenic, my friend's mother was diagnosed with bipolar illness. When I last saw her, she was stable and in a normal mood. What the mother always wanted was acceptance, understanding, and unconditional love, and she got these from her family and a few friends. But most of the time, she was misunderstood by those who knew her least.

Q-149. My adult child recently has been diagnosed with bipolar disorder. I made many mistakes as a parent, and I wonder if my actions caused the illness. Now I feel that I might have been a bad parent. Was I?

I don't know you well enough to have an opinion on that, but your behavior as a parent did not cause your child's illness. Remember, bipolar disorder has its roots in your child's genes. You could have been a good parent or a bad parent or have not even been around, and this illness probably would have happened anyway.

After this illness has started with either a manic or a major depressive episode, the possibility exists that you handled the situation using poor judgment. Think through *your* actions (not your child's actions) with honesty and see if *you* have done anything wrong. If you feel that you have done something wrong, go to your son or daughter and make amends wherever wise and possible. If your son or daughter has wronged you, your child's responsibility is for making his or her own amends. We make many mistakes when we don't have all the facts about this illness, and much misunderstanding is usual. Nobody handles it perfectly, and people's rights, wishes, and dreams get stepped on. Remember, making mistakes or doing bad things out of ignorance doesn't make you a bad person.

Q-150. I constantly am doing "everything" for my daughter who has bipolar illness, and she has told me to stop it. What am I doing wrong?

Most people with bipolar illness want the same control over their life as they did before the illness, and they want to function normally in every way.

Your daughter is the same person that she was before the illness began; her hopes and dreams of a normal, functional life are still within her. By doing everything for her, you are reinforcing the idea that she is helpless and very different than she was before the illness, and she may be very capable of managing her own life. Just give her time to adjust to the changes brought on by the illness. Here are some guidelines for a family member (or even a friend) that might help you.

1. Do not meddle or intervene in their personal lives unless their doctor has recommended that you do so.
2. Do not attempt to control any facet of their lives.
3. Ask them whether they want your assistance; do not assume they need it.
4. Let them do for themselves all that they are able. Do not do for them what they are able, yet unwilling, to do for themselves.
5. Let them suffer the consequences of their own actions and decisions except when life threatening.
6. Let them live their own life with their own dreams and goals.
7. Do not allow unhealthy dependencies to form.
8. Do not try to cure, heal, or fix them.
9. If you have concerns over something they are doing, discuss it with them, and accept their decision.

Q-151. When I visit someone in a psychiatric hospital, how should I act?

You should be yourself because the person with bipolar illness doesn't want you to change because of their illness. Knowing that you are the same person before and after their hospitalization is important. Because the person could feel lousy due to the side effects of medication, try not to be overbearing, argumentative, talkative, or judgmental. Most importantly, listen, give assurance, tell them you still care, and treat them as a friend or family member who happens to have a medical illness rather than a mental illness. Talking about common interests, hobbies, or fun things that you have done with the hospitalized person will help them to feel that they are still in touch with themselves. Be balanced in your conversation and don't be negative; talk about the way they feel, and talk about things unrelated to hospitalization. Finally, don't become part of the problem by yielding to the person's requests to help them escape from the hospital, for bringing other medications from home to the hospital, and for anything else that is contrary to the doctor's treatment plan for that individual.

Q-152. Will my family member with the illness ever have a normal life?

These days, what is a normal life? In my view, possible components of a normal life are having no more symptoms of the illness, having no side effects from medication, having great friends, having good relations with relatives, working full-time, supporting oneself, being productive, making one's life count, pursuing hobbies and interests, being in love, having healthy children, having financial stability, being happy, and being a whole person.

Seldom do I meet anyone, with or without bipolar illness, who could claim a normal life by this definition. Who is to say whether one life is better than another? Why compare one life with another when each has its own valid purpose in this world at this point in time? Everyone has problems and obstacles to overcome, and no one lives a problem-free perfect life. I have met people with bipolar illness who have many of these components of a "normal" life, and your family member may attain them too. Just because his or her life has deficits from "normality" this year, doesn't mean that he or she will have them in 5 or 10 years. Time and effort are required to climb the bipolar mountain and conquer the related obstacles. Give your family member love and support and be patient; accept your family member where he or she is today. His or her life is still "under construction" and isn't finished yet.

Q-153. I don't know how to act around my friend who was recently diagnosed with bipolar illness. Sometimes I want to keep my distance, and other times I want to have fun like we used to in years past. How should I view my friend now?

When I was a kid, I had a very good friend who was mentally retarded. I saw very quickly that he had two sides to him. One was the friend with whom I played, and the other was the effects of being mentally retarded. I knew who my friend was (the person), and I always saw that part of him rather than his retardation (the illness). The years of friendship with him made it easier for me to accept people with mental and behavioral abnormalities today and to accept myself. Here are some guidelines that I have learned that might help you.

1. Look deeper into your friend; go beyond the symptoms of the illness and identify the true person you've known as a friend.
2. Identify the moods, and behavior that are typical for your friend's bipolar illness and view them as the illness.
3. Get as much education as you can to help you understand the illness. This will help you separate your friend from the illness.
4. Imagine temporarily that your friend has diabetes instead of bipolar illness. Your friend didn't choose to become diabetic, but the symp-

toms can be treated with medication. People have diabetes, and they function well if they live by certain health guidelines. People don't stigmatize those with diabetes, and they don't need to for bipolar illness either because bipolar illness has physical or biological origins.

5. Give yourself and your friend some time to redefine your relationship and strengthen your friendship.

Love is an action, not just a feeling.

Q-154. How will my friends and family react to my illness?

In general, people will respond to the knowledge that you have bipolar disorder with the same response you give to having the illness. If you show fear and confusion, they'll be frightened and confused. If your attitude is one of hopelessness and helplessness, your friends and family will be alarmed and discouraged. If you choose the role of a victim, they'll feel victimized. But if you are calm, collected, and show the resolve to overcome the illness, friends and family will also be calm, positive, and optimistic. People react to our attitudes and actions, and positive attitudes will yield a positive response in our friends and family.

Someone can give you an initial negative reaction no matter how good your response to the illness is. If you are around this person frequently, you can show them that you are still the same person you used to be by your actions, comments, and attitudes. You can demonstrate to them that you are not "damaged goods" and something to be shunned. Over a period of time, you have a good probability of winning back the few friends or family members that drifted away.

Q-155. Will my friends still like me?

If your illness has been around for some time, I think your friends will still accept you if you choose to tell them that you have bipolar disorder. Your friends know what your behavior is like, and they already accept you the way you are. Why should they dislike you for naming (bipolar) or labeling the behavior (depression and mania) they already know about? The friends who have seen the best and worst of you will stick with you.

If your illness has just started, some friends may have a difficult time continuing their friendship with you. Your friends will probably have as much difficulty understanding what you're going through as you have in understanding what you're going through. Remember, this new experience has changed you in some respects. The illness is a tool that transforms us and has the potential to deepen our character. If your friends aren't ready or willing to walk down that deeper path, they may choose to leave you; however, some of your friends may want a friend who has a depth of character forged by this illness. One thing is for sure, all your friendships will be modified as a result of the recent onset of bipolar disorder because *you* have changed. Think about the following questions. Do you have to tell your friends that you have a bipolar disorder? Have they seen your mood changes, and do you need to give them a reason for them? What do you expect to gain by telling your friends? If you tell a friend, can you bear the consequences of losing him or her or changing the relationship? All these questions are hard, but they should be thought through. You'll make some mistakes, but in the end you have the potential for deeper, more open relationships than most people.

> A friend is someone
> who understands your past,
> believes in your future,
> and accepts you today
> just the way you are.

Q-156. Over the course of my illness, I have argued and said some mean things to a friend. How do I straighten out my relationship?

From my own experience, apologizing for the things I said or did usually wasn't enough. Instead, making amends for the wrongs I did was necessary. What are amends? Amends are the actions I take to right the wrongs that I have caused in a relationship, and they include making restitution for the damage done, pain inflicted, abuse given, or things taken. When I make amends for something I did, it clears my mind and soul of the wrong. Amends making benefits me as well as the friend who was wronged, and I must do it for *my* mental health. In the process of making amends, I'm not to look at the wrongs that my friend did to me because my friend is responsible for making amends for those wrongs; making amends for my wrongs is my responsibility. A friend might not accept my amends, but I have done my part to straighten out the relationship; that's all that I can do.

Steps for Making Amends

1. Get your "heart" right so that you are able to honestly identify the wrongs you did to your friend. Removing any denial is a must.

2. Make a written list of the wrongs you did.
3. Become willing to make amends for the wrongs you did.
4. Judge whether making amends would add more injury or harm to your friend. If this is the case, don't make amends.
5. Make direct amends to your friend. Direct means face to face if possible.

Your friend or family member
might be wanting to repair the relationship too,
but not know how.

PR-12. A PSYCHIATRIST'S RESPONSE

The family and friends of the patient with bipolar illness are vital to the successful treatment of his or her disorder. As mentioned before, man is a social animal. We need one another from the time we enter this world as new born infants until the time we are grieved over in a ritual and ceremony marking our transition from this life to the one hereafter. Patients with bipolar disorder need help with their illness just as diabetic patients, patients with high blood pressure, or those with any other affliction need help from family and friends.

Specifically, what does someone with bipolar disorder need from their family and friends? Mostly, family and friends need to address and confront their own feelings about their family member or friend who has a stigmatizing disorder. Although there have been considerable advances in the way our society and culture deals with mental illness and bipolar disorder, a strong odor of bigotry, prejudice, and fear of individuals with a mental disorder still lingers. So one of the first things that families and friends need to do is to recognize the stigma that the illness carries. Be aware of the fears that the patient will have concerning the behaviors of manic, hypomanic, or major depressive episodes. I know that confronting feelings is difficult, and even a psychiatrist easily feels uncomfortable with the patient who is "on the ceiling," and threatening and posturing in a frightening way.

The patient may fear rejection and abandonment by friends and family. The proper response should be an immediate and forceful acknowledgement of your feelings about this disorder and your willingness not to reject or abandon the patient. Family and friends will find it easier to discuss this issue than for the one who has the disorder. So don't be afraid to address openly the symptoms and issues that surround the bipolar disorder, thus showing the patient that you are not afraid of the individual nor do you intend to reject him or her. To accomplish this, family and friends should learn everything they can about this bipolar disorder. Nothing is more reassuring for an individual with this disorder than to have others who know about his or her problem and who care and support that individual.

Support groups are available for family and friends of those with bipolar illness. Support groups are a rich source of information and support for family and friends as well as the bipolar individual. Understanding this disorder is much easier when it is explained by someone who has recovered from the symptoms. Individuals who have gone through a severe crisis with their bipolar disorder have suffered this experience which is transformational. They have become a new and different individual in some respects, but obviously they are basically the same person. There must be an acknowledgement and acceptance of these changes so that the patient's acceptance of his or her new status is supported. Remember that recovery is a process, and a very important factor for those involved is patience.

The recovery from the extreme expressions of this disorder takes considerable time for some. Patients may have to stay in convalescent homes or halfway houses for a period of weeks or months while they slowly gain back their sense of self and their ability to manage in their environment.

What kinds of changes do you notice? Hopefully, the patient's moods have been stabilized. Mood swings are one of the major characteristics of bipolar disorder, and when these mood swings stop or are modulated, the patient, family, and friends have to adjust to this new positive change.

During recovery, how do you explain the changes in the patient's lifestyle to his or her other family members and friends or to more distant friends? The patient now is taking perhaps several medications. He or she may be going to support groups, seeing a psychiatrist on a regular basis, and going in and out of hospitals. They may be recently unemployed or unable to drive as in previous times. He or she may have had to drop out of school and other meaningful activities. All of these issues are major, and the patient needs help from family and friends to successfully deal with these many issues.

Fortunately, no patient and no family or friend must deal with this illness alone. Support groups are available in every major city. Don't hesitate to contact your doctor for help or call your county mental health association for the resources in your community.

EMPLOYMENT
RELATED ISSUES

Note: Answers to legal questions that follow (Q-160 through Q-167) do not represent legal advice for your specific circumstances; your situation and related questions should be analyzed and discussed by legal counsel on an individual basis.

Q-157. I think that I have been discriminated against in my job because I have a bipolar disorder. Who will help me clarify my rights?

First, you should not assume that you know all the State and Federal laws that might have been broken because you may be aware of only a fraction of the laws. You should discuss your concerns with a labor law attorney, and you can find one by looking in the yellow pages of your telephone book under Attorneys, Labor Law. For more help, call your local branch of the National Alliance for the Mentally Ill for a referral. If you don't have much money, contact your local Legal Aid Society (in the white pages, under Business Listings). Also, your doctor or someone in a bipolar support group possibly could recommend an attorney. Talk to several attorneys and find one with whom you feel most comfortable. Tell them you have a bipolar disorder and describe the illness if necessary, and see if they are sympathetic to your needs. As with any profession, some attorneys are better than others; get their resume and look it over closely. Finally, I would advise you not to talk to company officials about your discrimination concerns unless your labor law attorney says to do so.

Q-158. What will a labor law attorney cost me?

Many labor law attorneys charge by the hour or a fraction of an hour, and I've found that experienced ones cost more per hour than my psychiatrist. Usually, they take a deposit or retainer before proceeding on a specified scope of work. When another phase of your legal work comes up, you'll be required to pay that retainer ahead of the work. Finding the money to finance your legal defense can be difficult, but if you have a good case, it's well worth it. When I was searching for a labor law attorney, I couldn't find one who would take my case based on a contingency or a percentage of a final settlement. Also, attorneys are more than willing to discuss their fee schedule; so discuss it at the start. Most of the time, you would probably recover the attorney's fees as part of a settlement.

Q-159. What will my labor law attorney and I go through to resolve the case?

Most attorneys will give you 10 or 15 minutes on the phone free to discuss whether your discrimination or employment concerns are valid. If your rights have been violated by your employer (or by an employee of the company), an attorney will inform you of your rights and give you several options for resolving the problem. You probably will have to decide whether you want to keep your job or not. This decision will affect the course of action chosen by your attorney.

Think of your attorney as your hired pit bull. Attorneys are paid to take the "heat" for you, and they will confront your company to argue and fight for you. Most likely, you won't have to face the company officials one-on-one; your attorney will do it for you.

If you have a moderate to good case, and your case cannot be resolved simply, you and your company are likely to enter into mediation rather than a court trial. Most discrimination cases end in a mediation and don't go to court. In a mediation, you and your attorney would usually be in a separate room from your company's officials and attorneys. Another neutral attorney, a mediator, would shuttle back and forth between the rooms giving proposals and counter proposals. The goal of a mediation would be to reach a mutually agreeable settlement, usually monetary, and avoid a more costly and stressful court battle. The overall process from the time you first talk to your attorney and the time of the settlement usually takes a minimum of several months.

Through the whole process, you will learn a great deal. You may make mistakes, and your attorney may not provide you with all the options. So I encourage you to ask many questions, and make sure your attorney is representing you competently and efficiently.

Q-160. When is it legal for a *potential* employer to ask about my medical history?

It is unlawful for an employer to ask general questions about your physical condition on an application form, pre-employment questionnaire, or in the course of the recruitment and hiring process. Examples of prohibited inquiries include questions regarding particular disabilities, treatment for diseases or conditions, and Workers' Compensation claims.

It is lawful, however, for an employer to ask questions about an applicant's medical history if questions are directly related to the job position. For example, an employer could ask you if you had any health problems that would keep you from performing their job requiring intensive physical labor. Also, questions can be asked regarding whether the applicant would endanger their health and safety or the health and safety of others.

An employer could outline major job duties and then question applicants as to whether or not they can perform these duties with or without an accommodation.

After an offer of employment has been made, an employer may condition employment upon satisfactory results of a post offer medical examination or medical inquiry if this is a requirement for all entering employees in the same job category. This examination or inquiry does not have to be job related and may encompass questions about a potential employee's medical history. If the potential employee is not hired after this medical examination because it reveals a disability, the reason for refusing to hire that employee must be job related and necessary for the business. The employer also must show at that time that no reasonable accommodation is available or would enable this employee to perform the essential job functions, or that accommodation would impose an undue hardship.

Q-161. I have just started a new job. Is it ever legal for my new *current* employer to ask about my medical history?

Once employed, any medical examination or inquiry required of an employee must be job related and justified by business necessity. Exceptions are voluntary examinations conducted as part of employee health programs and examinations required by other federal laws. The information received from medical inquiries may not be used to discriminate against an employee.

Q-162. If an employer or potential employer questions me about my medical history in violation of the law, how should I answer them?

Each situation is different, but the applicant or employee might wish to inform the employer that, according to the Americans With Disabilities Act, the question is inappropriate and therefore the applicant or employee need not answer the question.

Q-163. What is accommodation and when is it required?

Reasonable accommodation is any change in the work environment or in the way things are usually done that results in an equal employment opportunity for an individual with a disability. An employer must make a reasonable accommodation to the known physical or mental limitations of a qualified applicant or employee with the disability unless it can be shown that the accommodation would cause an undue hardship on the operation of its business.

Reasonable accommodation may include job restructuring, part-time or modified work schedules, reassignment to a vacant position, acquisition or modification of equipment or devices, appropriate adjustment or modifications of examinations, training materials or policies, the provision of qualified readers or interpreters, and other similar accommodations for individuals with disabilities.

Q-164. If I want accommodation, whom do I have to tell at my place of employment that I have bipolar disorder?

If a job applicant or employee has a hidden disability, it is their responsibility to make the need for an accommodation known. If an applicant or an employee requests an accommodation, and the need for the accommodation is not obvious, the employer may request documentation of the individual's limitations to support the request. All medical related information must be kept confidential. There are some exceptions: (a) supervisors and managers may be informed about restrictions on the work or duties of an employee and necessary accommodations, (b) first aid and safety personnel may be informed if the disability might require emergency treatment or if any specific procedures are needed in the case of fire or other evacuations, and (c) relevant information may be provided to insurance companies where the company requires a medical examination to provide health or life insurance for employees.

Q-165. I'm a part-time employee with a limit to the length of my employment. Do I have the same rights as a regular full-time employee with respect to my employer having to make accommodation for my illness?

Part-time employees are covered to the same extent as full-time employees under the Americans With Disabilities Act. The fact, however, that an employee is part-time may have some impact on the determination of whether an accommodation is reasonable or creates an undue hardship for a business.

Q-166. I have only been working for a few months and have just been diagnosed with bipolar disorder; I'm also in an initial probationary period. Am I entitled to the same disability discrimination rights as a person who has been there a number of years?

Assuming that the individual meets the definition of an "individual with a disability" (a bipolar disorder qualifies), that person is entitled to the same disability discrimination rights as an employee who has been with the company for a number of years.

Q-167. My employer gave me a medical form to fill out. There was a question about ever having a mental illness. I lied to the employer and said that I never had a mental illness. Months have passed. Through some other way, my employer has just found out that I lied about having a mental illness. Can I be fired?

The employer may not discriminate against an employee because of the disability; however, the employer may be able to terminate the employee because of dishonesty. The employer must treat all employees the same regardless of whether they have a disability or not. Therefore, if the employer would terminate any employee because of dishonesty on an application, the employer would be entitled to terminate the disabled employee to the same extent. If, however, the employer would not terminate other employees for dishonesty on this type of form, they may not terminate the individual with the disability. A complete analysis would require consideration of the employer's disciplinary policies or the collective bargaining agreement in place regarding the particular employee. Also, the law is unclear as to whether an employee lawfully can be fired for lying in response to a question that lawfully could not be asked in the first place.

Q-168. Should I let my supervisor or co-workers know about my illness?

The real question here is what do you expect to gain by telling others about your illness? Are you trying to find friends on the job because it is difficult to find them outside of the workplace? Are you trying to gain acceptance from others in place of accepting and loving yourself? Why is there a need to bring the knowledge of this illness into the workplace? Think about these questions in-depth if they apply.

If you do not want accommodation or special treatment for your bipolar disorder, I do not recommend telling your supervisor. Most supervisors don't know much about bipolar disorder. If they hear the word manic-depressive, they'll be frightened and monitor your behavior more intensely and more critically. Supervisors may pass on the knowledge of your illness to their superiors and other important people in your company. You could be passed over for a promotion to a supervisory spot although you are well qualified.

Similar problems result when co-workers find out about your illness; however, you may know a few individuals at work really well, and telling them about your illness may be safe. You then could have an ally or two to talk to when things aren't going so well. And being known for who you are by a few at work can give a sense of security and belonging. But choose people wisely, and tell others only when you have accepted the risk. If your attempt to open up to a co-worker went wrong, could you work with a prejudiced, judgmental co-worker?

Q-169. When I apply for medical insurance, should I be truthful and tell them I have bipolar disorder?

If you have just started a job and are filling out the initial medical insurance enrollment forms, be truthful. The insurance company then will know about your preexisting condition and probably will limit benefits for bipolar disorder for the first year or some time period. But if you say that you don't have any illness and immediately start submitting claims for bipolar illness, the insurance company could easily find out if you had this preexisting illness by contacting your doctor; then you would be in big trouble. And remember, being honest on these forms won't get you fired.

If you are not employed and decide to get private medical insurance, being truthful about your illness most probably will result in a denial for insurance coverage. I won't tell you to lie about having a bipolar disorder, but being dishonest appears to be the only way to get medical insurance. If you lie about your illness and get insurance, you should never submit claims for bipolar illness related expenses. If the insurance company investigates your medical background after submitting a "bipolar" expense, you may be found out. If you are operated on, the records will show your medications and perhaps visits by your psychiatrist; "covering up" becomes complicated. You know what is at stake; the decision is yours. Let us all hope, that in the future, medical insurance won't be denied to those with preexisting conditions.

Q-170. What is a health reimbursement account?

Many companies have a health reimbursement account as part of their overall medical benefit program. The advantage of this program is that the money you put into the program is counted as nontaxable income. For many, this is the only way to get a reduction in taxes for medical expenses that weren't reimbursed. Most of our non-reimbursed medical expenses don't exceed the minimum amount to qualify as an itemized deduction, but this program gives us another way to get a tax break.

You can designate a yearly amount to be put into the account, and this amount would be equally deducted from your paychecks throughout the year. You should figure the amount of medical, dental, and other qualified expenses that won't be reimbursed by your insurance for expenses like deductibles and coinsurance. Be sure that you will spend all that is in your account because any that is left at the end of a year will be kept by the government. When you have qualified expenses, you submit a form and are reimbursed out of your account.

As an example, say that you have only put in $100 into your account by mid-March of a given year. The total that you are going to put into your account for the year is $600. In mid-March you have $250 worth of qualified expenses. Although you have only $100 in your account, you will be paid the whole $250 because you would have put in $600 by year's end. The health reimbursement account is another way of financing and preparing for those expected and unexpected medical expenses.

With the health care system constantly in change, it is not certain that this program will be part of a future system. As a good practice, talk to your employer and see if this program or other similar programs are available that will help you save money on your medical expenses.

PR-13. A PSYCHIATRIST'S RESPONSE

Work is an important aspect of most adult life. Obviously, your co-workers and your supervisors will know that you have been ill because you have been absent from work. They will be curious and they may even be a bit apprehensive, or even frightened, especially if they have little knowledge of mental illness and specifically about bipolar disorders. Bigotry and prejudice nearly always are caused by ignorance and fear.

Your responsibility is to help your co-workers and your supervisor understand your disorder and the problems it causes. I do not mean that you should go up to everyone and say, "I have a bipolar disorder, and this is what it does to me." If your illness does not cause a problem for you at work, and discussion is not appropriate between you and your supervisor or with co-workers, then you should feel comfortable in saying nothing about your illness. Co-workers and supervisors have no need to know that you have this illness unless you left work because of the illness, or because you want them to know you in a more intimate and realistic manner.

You might want accommodations made at work because of your illness. If some aspect of your work is particularly stressful, and you feel it is a major aggravation for your disorder and will hinder your recovery, you have the responsibility to ask for such accommodation. You should expect that your wishes will be respected in accordance with state and federal laws.

In my experience, nearly all of my patients with bipolar disorder have been able to return to work full-time. Some have had to leave the jobs because they were simply too stressful, and the job could not be modified so that they could handle it and remain well. For the most part, however, my patients have been able to return to work or school and do well and even thrive with the use of medication and therapy.

Those with this disorder find a new way of adapting to their careers, either by finding a new job or by making changes in their old job so that they find themselves more productive and much happier while working. A very important and necessary realization for patients with a bipolar disorder is that they are not crippled or permanently handicapped. They may have a disability, and they may need modifications of their work situations, but they have much to offer. In my experience, patients with a bipolar disorder who have recovered report they are happier and far more productive than they were before.

DISABILITY

Q-171. Should I purchase private disability insurance through my employer?

If for some reason, you become disabled and unable to work, private disability insurance will guarantee that your income will be 60% of your previous income. Without private insurance, Social Security and state disability combined may not provide near the 60% mark. So, if you can afford the insurance, get it.

Many of these private insurance policies have options of 30-, 90-, or 180-day waiting periods after you go on disability before benefits are paid. Again, select a waiting period that you can live with financially. Also, most policies have a two-year limit for benefits for mental disabilities like bipolar disorder.

Many policies define a preexisting condition as a condition for which the policyholder has received medical treatment or services, taken prescribed drugs or medicines, or consulted a physician at any time during a period of time immediately preceding the effective date of the policy. If you have a preexisting condition, the private disability insurance most likely would not pay benefits until a certain period of time has elapsed since the policy was purchased. Go over all the fine print of any private disability insurance in-depth.

Q-172. What does a typical private long-term disability policy give me for this illness in terms of money?

Once the waiting period has passed, a typical policy will pay you 60% of your normal monthly income from your job, and benefits usually are limited to

137

a two-year period. If you get Social Security in addition to your private insurance benefits, an amount equal to your Social Security benefits is usually deducted from your private insurance benefits. Sixty percent might not seem enough, but remember that much of Social Security benefits may be nontaxable depending on your total income. Most private insurance benefits are taxable, but this should be verified with your insurance company or tax consultant.

Q-173. I'm having a hard time doing my job because of my bipolar illness. Should I go on disability?

If you are unable to do your job at all, you should consider going on disability. In partnership with your doctor, this decision should be made. The following are some additional comments and questions to consider while making your decision to go on disability.

1. Do not quit your job. Choose to go on disability, and do it as described in Q-174. Or, if you can work reduced hours, do so. Your company is required to make accommodation for your illness; see Q-163.
2. If you think you are going to be fired because of some "bipolar behavioral problems" at work and could qualify for disability, go on disability rather than being fired and losing your disability insurance. (Also, see Q-174 and consider Q-157.)
3. Can you afford to go on disability?
4. Do you have insurance that pays benefits for partial disability?
5. How will being disabled affect your future employment potential?
6. How will you cope with being unemployed?

Q-174. How do I go on disability?

First, you and your doctor must decide that you are disabled by your bipolar disorder and no longer able to perform the duties of your job. If you are currently employed, let your supervisor know that you will be out sick for a week due to your doctor's orders. Next, call the benefits department of your company and tell them that your doctor has put you on disability and request the necessary disability paperwork. You want to leave no doubt that your decision to go on disability has been ordered by your doctor and is not just a convenient escape route from the workplace. Examples of paperwork that you should receive depending on which options you choose with your company are (a) long-term disability insurance and (b) short-term disability insurance that usually fills the gap or waiting period required by the long-term insurance. You also might request a supply of medical insurance forms.

Whether you are employed or not, call the Social Security Administration and get an application for benefits (Social Security Disability and Supplemental Security Income) as soon as you are disabled. Look in the telephone book in the government pages, under U.S. Government Offices, Health & Human Services, Social Security Administration. Because there is a waiting period of five or six months from the time you apply for Social Security Disability, the sooner you get the paperwork in, the sooner the benefits come.

Q-175. How easy is it to get disability benefits?

To be considered as disabled under Social Security, you must be unable to do any kind of work for which you are suited, and your inability to work must last at least a year. When applying for Social Security benefits, it is not uncommon for them to deny first-time claims to those with a mental illness. Unless you have a history of bipolar illness documented by several doctors, they may choose to deny your claim. If your bipolar illness has just started, you may have to make more of an effort to prove that you are disabled by obtaining the opinions of several doctors. If your claim is denied, you have a right to appeal your case through four levels of appeal. Since the last stage of appeals includes a hearing before a judge, it would be wise to get an attorney who specializes in Social Security Law to represent you if your claim has been denied. You can find one by looking in the yellow pages of your telephone book under Attorneys, Social Security Law.

Applying for benefits from a private disability insurance company requires the same detailed effort of filling out forms and providing documentation. Because an appeals process may be limited, you should make sure that your application carries enough substantial documentation of your disability to get through their approval process without any questions. If you have little or no history of bipolar illness or any mental illness, getting a second opinion from another psychiatrist may be wise. Insurance companies may argue with one doctor's opinion, but they are much less likely to challenge your claim for benefits if you have several doctors all saying you are disabled.

When private insurance companies, state agencies, and Social Security request information from you, giving them exactly what they want is very important. Included are filling out all forms in every detail and being available to answer any questions. Making special trips to your doctor to get forms filled out and signed may be necessary. If you don't play exactly by the rules, your claim for benefits could be denied or slowed down. Be sure to make copies of all forms and documentation that you provide.

Q-176. What is SSI?

SSI stands for Supplemental Security Income and is provided by the Social Security Administration. It provides income for those disabled by bipolar disorder as well as other disabilities; also, people who get SSI usually get food stamps and Medicaid. If you already have significant income from other sources or own a lot of things, you may not qualify for SSI.

Contact the Social Security Administration to find out the latest details on this program. Whether you think you qualify or not, apply for SSI right away if you're disabled because of bipolar disorder. If qualified, SSI will start the day you apply, not the day you became disabled.

Q-177. Can Medicare help pay my medical bills?

Medicare is a Federal health insurance program for the disabled (and elderly) regardless of income and assets. (Medicaid is a medical assistance program financed by the government for eligible low-income individuals.) Anyone who has been entitled to Social Security disability benefits for more than 24 months is eligible for Medicare. Medicare coverage is divided into two parts:

(a) Part A insurance is basically hospitalization insurance and covers inpatient care, and no premium is charged for those already on Social Security disability. Part A helps pay for up to 190 days of inpatient care in a psychiatric hospital during a beneficiary's lifetime. Psychiatric care in general hospitals, rather than in exclusively psychiatric hospitals, is not subject to this 190-day limit. The deductible was $716 per benefit period in 1995. The Part A deductible applies to each benefit period, and you may have to pay more than one deductible in a year if you are hospitalized more than once in the benefit period.

(b) Part B insurance covers outpatient care such as visits to a doctor, but most outpatient prescription drugs are not yet covered. Part B insurance cost $46.10 per month in 1995, and the deductible was $100 per year. Medicare pays 80% of approved charges for covered services after the deductible has been met. Medicare has a set amount per geographic location that it will pay for a specific service, but your doctor may charge more than the set amount.

There is private health insurance designed specifically to supplement Medicare's benefits by filling the gaps in Medicare's coverage. For more information on this subject, read the *Guide to Health Insurance for People with Medicare* that is referenced below.

If you want to know more about Medicare, I recommend obtaining the following free publications:

The Medicare Handbook
Medicare Q&A 85 Commonly Asked Questions
Guide to Health Insurance for People with Medicare
Medicare and Coordinated Care Plans
Medicare and Other Health Benefits
Medicare and Your Physician's Bill
Medicare Savings for Qualified Beneficiaries

The publications can be obtained from any Social Security office or write for them at the following address:

Medicare Publications
Health Care Financing Administration
6325 Security Boulevard
Baltimore, MD 21207

It took me 54 days to receive these publications by writing to the above Baltimore address.

PR-14. A PSYCHIATRIST'S RESPONSE

An important understanding for my patients to have is that being disabled is not a crime, not something to be ashamed of, and feel they are in an inferior position in society. Simply, disability is a realistic appraisal of one's life and circumstances at a particular point in time. If your doctor decides that you are disabled and unable to work because of your illness, I hope you have the good sense to accept that as a reasonable solution to your problem for that time. Disability does not have to be permanent. You very likely will be able to overcome the disabling parts of your illness and be willing and able to return to work at a future date.

Keeping in mind that you have paid for disability insurance is valuable. Those disabled by bipolar illness are entitled to Social Security disability benefits or other benefits paid for by additional insurance. Insurance is the way our society, like most other civilized societies, strives to help individuals who have become disabled because of illness or injury. Failure to go on disability when you need to is one of the main hindrances for getting well. Going on disability is an acceptable option in the overall treatment of bipolar illness.

Your physician or therapist has the responsibility to help you deal with your feelings about being on disability. Your doctor should help you understand that your illness is not your fault, that negative attitudes and feelings are understandable but not helpful, and that feelings of embarrassment, shame, and humiliation are neither useful nor necessary in helping you deal with your disorder. Your doctor or therapist will help you change your thoughts and your beliefs, and subsequently your behaviors and feelings about being disabled will change.

HOSPITALIZATION

Q-178. I have heard "horror stories" about the treatment of the mentally ill in psychiatric hospitals many years ago. This past week I was surprised to read that violations of several patients' rights continue in one modern psychiatric hospital. How are modern psychiatric hospitals different from those of 20 or 30 years ago?

"Horror stories" can happen in any hospital, but they are the exception, not the rule. Where do most people get their ideas about mental or psychiatric hospitals? They get them from movies, television documentaries, television news, and newspapers. But many people think hospitals are like those depicted in movies such as "One Flew Over the Cuckoo's Nest" where people in white suits run around saying "you're not going anywhere" or trying to provoke the patients. For the people who watch these kinds of TV shows, I suggest that they think about how Hollywood portrays their own professions. You'll find that Hollywood has much more of a need for drama and sensationalism than for reality. Have you ever watched a TV show about a topic where you really knew the facts? I'm sure you saw some distortions and artistic license in the program. When the same kind of thing is done to hospitals and the mentally ill, it scares people; this is a real disservice to the mentally ill. Those actions promote stigma, and stigma prevents people from getting help.

Twenty or thirty years ago, many of the medicines we have today were not available, and they used physical restraints instead. Hospital personnel had to tie up people who were running around hurting other people within the hospital. With the advent of psychotropic medications 30 to 35 years ago, hospitals began to use these drugs as chemical restraints. With more patients under control or restrained due to medication, hospitals could have smaller staffs and need less mechanical restraint. If a person is violent today, a danger to themselves or others, they may still be restrained or put in a padded seclusion room. As soon as they are nonviolent, they would be let loose according to the rules and regulations for restraining people.

In some parts of the country, mental hospitals are still comparatively primitive. State hospitals are better than they used to be, but they're still not as advanced as the private hospitals and some non-profit hospitals. Some hospitals may have those older undesirable traits; but as a whole, they are very closely regulated. Patients' rights advocates keep people from being held against their will, and they also come in and check records. For more on patient's rights, read *Rights of the Mentally Disabled, Statements and Standards* (American Psychiatric Association, Hospital and Community Psychiatry Service, 1988). Also, a local branch of the National Alliance for the Mentally Ill (Phone 703-524-7600; FAX 703-524-9094) can inform you of some of the mental health laws in general, and tell you how to contact a patient advocacy program.

When I see pictures of hospitals years ago, the old hospitals look like prisons compared to modern hospitals. Many people think that they are going to enter a hospital and find people wearing white coats. In many psychiatric hospitals it would be difficult to tell the difference between the hospital staff and the patients by their appearance. If you want to know exactly what a psychiatric hospital looks like inside, or how it functions, or have your fears calmed about hospitalization, visit a hospital and have them give you a tour. You have every right to know what the interior of a hospital looks like as well as how it functions. Ask as many questions as you want to feel informed and comfortable about the hospital and its staff.

Q-179. How do I find a good psychiatric hospital?

First, if a hospital does all 13 items in the following list, I would consider it a good hospital. If the hospital refuses to do Items 3 through 13 prior to admission, you don't want to be there. After admission, the hospital should do all items.

1. The doctors and hospital staff communicate openly with you and provide information at all times. Obviously, they can't tell you a lot about

your particular needs and treatment until you are hospitalized and diagnosed.

2. Symptoms of the illness and side effects of medication are discussed with the patient, family, and friends.
3. A general treatment plan is discussed to give you an idea of what is available for treatment, what is going to be done psychologically, and what is going to be done biologically or chemically.
4. With their experience, they give you a reasonable time limit estimate for your length of stay.
5. They have after-care or day-care programs and some free self-help support groups.
6. The frequency of visits by a psychiatrist will be told to you.
7. Your questions are answered about what a hospital is and how it functions.
8. You get answers for your unknowns.
9. You are allowed to take a tour of the hospital.
10. You should be allowed to speak to one of the clinical staff and ask what is going on.
11. You should get reasonable answers for all of your questions.
12. They can promptly provide you with their Patient's Rights Handbook or similar publication.
13. They have a good reputation and no history of abuse towards patients. You might have to investigate to get results on this item; check with patient rights advocates in your location.

To get a clear idea of the costs associated with hospitals, talk to the marketing department within the hospital first. A fee schedule should be provided by the hospital, and they should do an insurance check to see if the stay will be covered and to what degree. An understanding about costs should be in place before admittance. If you can't go to a particular hospital because of finances, the hospital should refer you to one that will.

The length of stay in a hospital should be based on the need for symptom reduction, not a fixed number of days set by an insurance policy. The treatment plan has to be reasonable based on your symptoms, not on how much insurance you have.

To make a short list of hospitals for your later evaluation, ask for recommendations or references from members of a bipolar support group or your psychiatrist. As a second approach, search in the telephone book yellow pages under hospitals. To choose your hospital, compare each alternative with facts found about the 13 items listed previously.

Q-180. When should I be hospitalized for bipolar illness?

When any one or more of the following three conditions occurs, you should be hospitalized.

1. When you are a danger to yourself.
2. When you are a danger to someone else.
3. When your judgment is impaired to the point where you cannot provide yourself with food, shelter, and clothing.

By recognizing the first symptoms of a mood episode and promptly getting to your doctor for psychological and/or biological intervention, you may avoid hospitalization. If you go past the point where insight isn't working to solve your escalating symptoms, someone should try to get you to the hospital.

Q-181. What are the requirements to have a friend or relative involuntarily committed to a psychiatric hospital?

One of the three conditions for hospitalization mentioned in Q-180 must be met. Then you can try to reason with the person and get them to a hospital. If their mood is extremely depressed, they may follow your lead. If they are extremely manic, they probably won't listen to reason. If reason doesn't work, the next step is calling the police and telling them what is going on. The police have to take them in for an evaluation at a hospital.

The rights of all patients are protected by law. If you are not a threat to yourself or someone else, and you can provide food, shelter, and clothing, you can't be thrown into a hospital by the police. If, however, there is reason to suspect that one or more of the three conditions for hospitalization is met, the police could bring you to a hospital on a 72-hour hold. During that 72-hour period, the person has a right to a hearing where they could demonstrate that they can provide food, shelter, and clothing, and that they're not a threat to themselves or someone else. If these things are demonstrated, the person would have to be turned loose. Once a person is placed involuntarily in a hospital, the person is not the hospital's captive; there are laws safeguarding the person's rights.

Q-182. As an inpatient at a modern psychiatric hospital, what would I be doing?

After admittance to the hospital, blood and lab work are done to make sure that nothing other than a psychiatric illness is occurring. An evaluation is done to see if you are on any other medicines like heart medicine, blood pressure medicine, steroids, "street" drugs of which some could mimic manic or depressive symptoms, and other medicines that may cause symptoms of mania and depression. Other illnesses have to be ruled out like metabolic illnesses and endocrine disorders. After all of these have been ruled out, they could give you antimanic drugs, antipsychotic drugs, and/or antidepressants. When your insight starts to come back, you are taught coping skills and how to identify early warning signs of depression and mania. A big part of your treatment includes a cognitive component—that is, learning a new way of thinking.

Some of the types of groups in a day's schedule may include the following: groups for helping process emotions and feelings, assertiveness groups, relationship groups, relaxation and breathing exercises group, art therapy group for insight, psychodrama group for saying good-bye to a loved one, a group to practice talking to a family member about an important issue, and a group for learning coping and adapting skills.

Here is an actual schedule from a local hospital describing a very active day that looks like a lot of work. I think a schedule like this breaks all of society's preconceived ideas about what goes on in a modern psychiatric hospital.

Adult Inpatient Schedule—Weekdays

6:30 a.m.	Wake-up
7:15 –8:00 a.m.	Breakfast
8:15–8:30 a.m.	Community Meeting
8:30–9:30 a.m.	Anxiety Meeting
9:30–10:30 a.m.	Gym Time or Leisure Education or Medication Group or Abuse Recovery Program or Art Therapy
11:00–12:00 p.m.	Group for education, demonstration, inquiry for coping and adapting skills
12:00–12:45 p.m.	Lunch
12:45–1:00 p.m.	Free Time
1:00–1:50 p.m.	Nutrition Group or Relations Group or Journal Time
2:00–2:50 p.m.	Art Therapy or Relations Group or Co-dependency or Self-Esteem Group
3:00–4:00 p.m.	Community Group or Journal Time
4:00–4:30 p.m.	Free Time
4:30–5:00 p.m.	Community Meeting
5:00–6:00 p.m.	Dinner
6:00–7:00 p.m.	Visitation or Contact Time (one to one with a mental health counselor, nurse, clinical specialist) or Patient/Family Group

7:00–8:00 p.m.	Contact Time or Cognitive Therapy or After Care
8:00–9:00 p.m.	Reflections—group time to reflect on what was learned or experienced during the day
9:00–9:30 p.m.	Stress Management

A group activity or outing for two hours on a Saturday morning is common, and a two-hour movie on Saturday and Sunday nights is also typical.

PR-15. A PSYCHIATRIST'S RESPONSE

First, let me say that I am not a hospital doctor. I do not put patients in the hospital, and I don't treat patients while they are in the hospital. I do, however, have patients who need to go to the hospital and who need to be treated there. My role is crucial in helping patients understand why they should be in the hospital, what the hospital can do for them, and how to get the most out of their stay in the hospital.

I am not a hospital doctor because I don't have the time or energy to split between my patients who see me in my office and patients in the hospital. Generally, some psychiatrists hospitalize whereas many do not, only because they cannot find a satisfactory way of dividing their time and professional care to their patients.

How do I decide when a patient of mine must go to the hospital? This is a very basic question. Simply put, if the patient cannot take care of himself or herself and has no family who can meet the needs of that patient, that patient should go into the hospital. These patients usually are suffering from the extreme forms of bipolar disorder; they are manic, psychotic, or severely depressed. In these states, they are a danger to others or to themselves. They may, through their manic behavior, injure others or themselves. Or, if they are severely depressed, they may not be able to eat or sleep, or meet their very basic needs; then I recommend the patient go into the hospital.

The exact procedure for having a patient go into the hospital varies depending on the answers to two questions. Primarily, what resources does the patient have in family, friends, and finances? What kind of insurance does the patient have?

Once I have decided, in my professional opinion, this patient should go into the hospital, I have to convince him or her that this is the best treatment option. Convincing my patient is not always easy; however, I very seldom have to threaten or coerce a patient, although sometimes it is necessary.

Some of my patients vociferously refuse to consider hospitalization. For the most part, I have been able to convince them this is a wise and realistic way to treat their illness. Often, I use family and friends to encourage and support me in my recommendations. Generally, if family, friends, and the doctor are unanimous in their recommendation and their advice, the vast majority of patients willingly enter the hospital and receive the treatment they need.

A very few patients adamantly refuse hospitalization. We then have to ask the community for assistance, and it usually comes in the form of the police. If the police are advised that this patient is a danger to himself or herself or to others, they will come and take the patient, by force if necessary, to a facility where the patient is held for 72 hours or less so that the psychiatrist and staff can determine what is in the best interest of the patient. If the patient wants to leave and the doctors feel the patient is a danger to himself or herself or others, or is unable to care for himself or herself, then the matter is brought before a judge, and the judge decides. In my experience, the hearing has always been extraordinarily fair and impartial. The judge is definitely not a rubber stamp who automatically goes along with the doctors. In my experience, judges have been fair and reasonable, and have made every effort to protect the patient's rights.

When I was young, I remember seeing a horrifying movie depicting a psychiatric hospital called "The Snake Pit." Of course, like many others, I also have seen "One Flew Over the Cuckoo's Nest" and felt equally frightened. My experience of working and training in psychiatric hospitals, however, helped me understand hospitals in a much more realistic way.

In general, I found the doctors, nurses, and other staff members of psychiatric hospitals to be extraordinarily sensitive, caring, and aware of their patients' specific needs and problems. With the advent of modern medication and psychopharmacology, few patients remain in psychiatric hospitals for long periods of time. The vast majority of patients leave after a period of a few weeks when their symptoms have abated, when their medication has minimized their symptoms, and when they are no longer a danger to themselves or to others.

IT'S AN EMERGENCY—
SUICIDE

Q-183. How prevalent is suicide among people with bipolar disorder?

Studies done on those with bipolar disorder show that about one in six will die as the result of suicide. They also show that 25% to 50% attempt suicide, and women are more likely than men to attempt suicide.

Why do they kill themselves? I don't believe it's their attempt to get back at someone or retaliate. They simply want to stop feeling the immense pain associated with depression, and suicide accomplishes that quickly. Their ability to think is distorted and impaired, and their normal reasoning ability has disappeared. The pain of depression usually drives their behavior, not their intellect. For some, drugs and alcohol further reduce a person's ability to think clearly enough to seek help. Whatever the contributing cause, suicide is more understandable when you view it as a way to end the tortuous pain of an illness. Suicide is a final desperate act to end the pain of depression.

If you were in extreme continuous pain from some illness for a long period of time and believed there was nothing you could do about it, wouldn't you be strongly tempted to end your life? Many people would. When you compound the pain with the inability to reason, suicide is just waiting to happen. Some find a way to bear the pain and keep seeking answers, and eventually they find relief from depression. For those who reach out for help, relief from the symptoms of the illness are abundant and very effective. Suicide is totally unnecessary because modern medicine can take away many or all the symptoms of depression. There are alternatives to suicide.

Q-184. What can I do to be more aware of the potential for suicide in a friend or family member with bipolar disorder?

1. Become very educated about bipolar illness.
2. Know the specific symptoms that the illness causes in your friend or family member.
3. Be able to spot changes in your friend or family, know what normal is for the following: moods, interests, behavior, daily routine, set of friends, and support structure.
4. Know the specific medications and amounts for your friend or family member including the range of possible side effects and the signs of overdose.
5. Ask the individual's doctor for an answer to your question.
6. Know what an intervention is and how to carry it out for your specific friend or family member.
7. Read *Suicide: Why? 85 Questions and Answers about Suicide* (Wrobleski, 1989), available through the NDMDA bookstore (Phone 312-642-0049; FAX 312-642-7243).

Q-185. Have you ever had someone threaten suicide?

Yes. I have known several, and my friendship with Richard was one occasion when I put to use everything I had learned and experienced. The experience gave me a sense of fulfillment because I used my past painful experiences to help another. Here is a true story about Richard with the key actions, points, and observations in bold.

Through some volunteer work I did with high school teens, I met a tall, slender 16-year-old named Richard. We spent time doing fun things like bicycling, canoeing, and going out to eat. Over a period of two months, I gained his **trust**. I built a "bridge" over which I could reach into Richard and **communicate** the deeper things of life. We started talking about the personal things in our lives, and by this process he learned that **I wasn't judgmental**.

One autumn day in October, 1985, Richard called me and told me that a 15-year-old neighbor friend killed himself several hundred feet from the back of Richard's house. Richard was upset and somewhat fearful that someone near his age could die. A week or so later, Richard called me and wanted to talk. He told me that he had a big drug problem and wanted help with it. He was a heavy marijuana smoker, and I had never seen any signs of it. I just thought that Richard was a funny, lively kid all on his own; I had no idea that he had been using drugs. I wasn't around him enough to see what his **normal behavior** was, and therefore, it was difficult to spot **abnormal or unusual behavior**. Richard said he was having a hard time with school, and this was unusual for him according to his mother. He said life seemed to be closing in around him; this was an unusual statement for any teenager.

The high school kids met weekly at one of the kid's homes for what we called "club." I picked up Richard at his house around 6:30 p.m. On the way to club, Richard surprised me and said that he was going to kill himself; he **made a suicidal statement or threat**. He said he had been thinking about suicide as a way out ever since his friend killed himself weeks earlier. I **identified with his feelings** because I once had suicidal thoughts and immense despair. Anytime someone says they are going to end it, I have been taught to **take him or her seriously**. I had to ask him **three questions**, and if he answered them all, he was surely serious about suicide. I asked, **"When are you going to do it?"** And he said, "midnight" of that night. I asked, **"Where are you going to do it?"** And he said, "in a [nearby uncompleted] house at the edge of the woods." I asked, **"How are you going to do it?"** And he said, "with my father's gun that I showed you a month ago." I **listened closely** and **spoke sensitively and compassionately** because I believed he was definitely suicidal.

At the club meeting, Richard was very quiet. After club, I told the club leader what Richard had said. **I got others involved. I knew that I should never leave a suicidal person alone, and I had to take him to help because I couldn't trust him to help himself.** I drove Richard home, and I told him that I needed to talk to his parents about this. I needed to **intervene** because Richard was a danger to himself. Richard worried about what they would say, and I said, "you were ready to kill yourself. Do you really care what they think?" He said no. I dropped Richard off at his friend's home across the street where his friend's parents watched him while I talked to Richard's parents.

I had anxiety as I knocked on the door to Richard's house. His mother answered, and I said that I needed to talk to her and Richard's father right away. In their family room, I told them that their son was a drug addict and was threatening suicide; we needed to get him to a hospital that night. It was no game. It was serious. They were almost speechless. They had come to respect me for the help I had given Richard over the previous two months, so they believed me.

I went across the street and brought Richard back to his house. I had to make all the decisions for him during this period because he wasn't thinking clearly. Richard was **looking for someone to follow** out of the nightmare because his depression had taken away his insight. The "club" leader showed up at Richard's house as Richard's father was calling a drug or psychiatric treatment hospital for adolescents. That night, Richard's father, the club leader, and I took Richard to a hospital at about 1:00 a.m.

The hospital program administrator said that if I hadn't helped Richard, he probably would have killed himself. The effort I put into Richard paid off. Within a week Richard was doing much better, and many barriers and obstacles that Richard had seen on that night came crashing down. He was facing his own problems, and there was communication in his family for the first time. For several weeks after he got out of the hospital, Richard idolized me, but then he began making other friends through his drug recovery program. After several months, Richard didn't want to spend any more time with me because he said I reminded him of his past. After that, I never heard from him again.

PR-16. A PSYCHIATRIST'S RESPONSE

The word suicide strikes terror in the hearts of family, friends, doctors, and therapists. Suicide is perceived by the suicidal individual as a valid way out of a very painful, seemingly impossible situation. The most important single piece of information that should always be kept in mind is to take all talk of suicide as serious. When a person talks about and thinks about suicide, he or she should be taken very seriously and helped.

How can you help someone who tells you he or she feels so bad that they are thinking of suicide? First of all, you should be aware that if the person tells you his or her thoughts, the patient is trusting you with his or her *feelings* and thoughts. If you listen to the person and encourage him or her to talk about his or her problems, fears, feelings, thoughts, and ideas, you will find that suicidal feelings diminish. It is highly likely that talking is the major way for individuals to lower arousal and to feel better; however, we may become so frightened at hearing suicidal talk that we do not listen to the individual. One must listen and listen very carefully; however, some suicidal individuals may be so depressed that their thought processes are distorted and reasoning is useless. For these individuals, you must get them professional help immediately.

If you are thinking of suicide and if you are thinking of how you are going to do it, when you are going to do it, and where you are going to do it, then you need to get help as quickly as possible. When you have gone that far in thinking about suicide, you are in much greater danger of carrying it out than if you merely have vague thoughts and ideas about suicide. If family and friends hear the patient talk about where, when, and how to attempt suicide, that family member and that friend must seek help immediately for their loved one. First, an intervention by the concerned family and friends is needed to take control of an individual who has lost his or her ability to make rational decisions. Second, the suicidal person must be taken by others to some mental health professional for help. Never assume that a suicidal person will seek treatment on his or her own! As the patient recovers, the suicidal thoughts diminish and disappear. Most patients do not think of suicide when their depression has lifted.

The suicidal patient must be observed carefully in the first few weeks of treatment. In a hospital setting, the staff is trained to watch for suicide attempts. If the patient is treated on an outpatient basis with medication, the first few weeks may be a very dangerous period. The medication energizes the patient before the suicide thoughts disappear. The patient then may have the energy to carry out plans of suicide. Creating a contract between patient and therapist or patient and friend or family is a frequently used technique to help the patient endure the painful period before the treatment takes effect. The patient can be queried daily as to how difficult it is to "keep the contract."

The responsibility of the psychiatrist or the mental health professional is to establish the attitude taken by friends and family. How observant must they be? What are the danger signs? Should the patient be hospitalized or not?

Even with the best of help and very careful monitoring, suicides still occur. Friends, family, and professionals all feel the terrible feeling of loss, sadness, and defeat.

ADDITIONAL RESOURCES

Q-186. Where can I find additional information on bipolar disorder and how to live with it?

1. In addition to the materials referenced in this book, the National Depressive and Manic-Depressive Association has over 80 titles in their Bookstore Catalog (Phone 312-642-0049; FAX 312-642-7243). Also, if you live near a university, check its medical library for material.
2. Local hospitals that sponsor support groups for people with bipolar disorder usually have many videotapes, movies, and audiotapes about the illness.
3. Of course, listening to the experiences of people with bipolar illness at support groups is a valuable type of education that you can't get elsewhere.
4. The Lithium Information Center has a great deal of information about the biomedical use of lithium and other treatments for bipolar disorder.

   Lithium Information Center
   Dean Foundation
   8000 Excelsior Drive, Suite 302
   Madison, WI 53717-1914
   Phone (608) 836-8070; FAX (608) 836-8033

5. The National Institute of Mental Health (NIMH) is the Federal agency that supports research nationwide on mental illness and mental health.

157

The Institute's Information Resources and Inquiries Branch responds to information requests from the public. These include printed materials on such subjects as removing the stigma of mental illness, the care of persons with severe mental illness, depression, bipolar disorder, seasonal affective disorder, and more. A list of NIMH publications, including several in Spanish, is available upon request.

National Institute of Mental Health
Information Resources and Inquiries Branch
5600 Fishers Lane, Room 7C-02
Rockville, MD 20857

Q-187. I have very little money and no insurance. Where can I go to get help for my bipolar illness?

Your county's department of mental health services exists to help those with bipolar illness (as well as other mental illnesses) who need care and treatment. In my county, anyone may receive mental health services regardless of how much money they have; most likely, your county has a similar arrangement. Contact them by looking in your phone book under Government Pages, County Government Offices, Mental Health Services, Referral & Info. The services most likely include crisis intervention, inpatient care, outpatient care, day treatment and socialization programs, continuing care, case management, medication monitoring, community outreach services to the homeless mentally ill, and services to people in jail. Additionally, since this "safety net" is usually strained by tight budgets or even budget cuts, some benefits and treatment options may be restricted to those with an acute illness.

The county psychiatric hospitals where I live admit only those who meet the legal criteria for involuntary commitment (see Q-181). If you want to be hospitalized for your distressing symptoms, you could be admitted voluntarily assuming you met the legal criteria for involuntary commitment. I suggest that you find out the rules for admission to your county's psychiatric facilities. Keep asking directions until you find the help you need. Don't give up!

THE LIGHT AT THE END
OF THE TUNNEL

(The following true story describes the change in my moods and the corresponding reactions to them during the first significant mood disturbance of my life. This story paints the common theme among those with a bipolar disorder that someone can function at a very good level in life, and literally overnight, a dramatic life-changing mood disorder can begin. Many find it hard to relate to the beginning of the illness, and they don't see the thoughts and feelings that a person with initial symptoms experiences. The story that follows gives an example of the thoughts and moods encountered during a first major depressive episode. The average person in our society is ignorant about bipolar illness, and this story helps correct many inaccurate, preconceived ideas. Many people with the illness, including their family and friends, have difficulty accepting the illness, but "The Light at the End of the Tunnel" shows that valuable insight can be a byproduct of wrestling with the illness. In conclusion, one may find a "silver lining" in the "cloud" of bipolar illness as I did, if one looks for it.)

Springtime was well under way in North Carolina as I began summer school in May, 1978. The warm and breezy season was my favorite time of year. The sky was bright blue and clear of the typical white haze of summer, and the sky made a perfect background for the new bright green of oaks and pines.

Exercise was one of my most favorite activities. I jogged several miles every other day, and I had run several ten-kilometer races. I had a membership at the downtown YMCA where I swam laps three times a week. In addition, I worked out at a health spa for two hours, three times a week on weight training machines. All this activity reinforced my confidence in my physical abilities, and exercising made me feel good about myself in general. I was 20 years old and had the youthful, I-can-do-anything spirit.

As summer school began, I had finished three years of a five-year Bachelor of Science program in Civil Engineering. My grades were excellent, and my GPA was over 3.75; I made the Dean's List every semester. I was astonished at how fast I could take exams; my mind worked as fast as lightning, which was normal for me. I was part of the co-op program where I worked a semester, then went to school for a semester. I had very few breaks with time for just myself.

It was another bright, breezy, summery day on the first day of June when my new friend Todd called and wanted me to go jogging with him. We met at the school gym already dressed for jogging. After stretching, we took off up the road by the gym and down by Western Boulevard. I felt really good and strong with a tremendous reservoir of strength, and I enjoyed the exercise and my new friend as I went over hill after hill.

Several times, Todd and I would go get an ice cold grape juice at the Student Union on campus and sit under a small shade tree and talk. Having friends meant a great deal to me, and even every little thing we did together, like drinking grape juice, was meaningful, fulfilling, and significant. The whole month of June seemed to be sunny, warm, and packed full of life; I was very alive, aware, and happy.

On a hot afternoon, Todd and I were running at a good pace down Hillsborough Street towards campus. I had my shirt off and felt so much power and energy as I glided up and over hills on a sidewalk that was old with broken segments sticking up in places. He was talking, but I wasn't paying much attention. My attention and thoughts were across the street, not with Todd or on my jogging. Not watching where I was going, my foot slipped off the edge of one of those pieces of concrete. Pain went through my foot as I put my whole weight and momentum on my twisted ankle. I tried to suppress my emotions and not express the pain to Todd or in public. Unwisely, I kept running, although slower and with a very noticeable limp.

Back in the locker room, I took off my shoe, and Todd and I inspected my right foot. I had greatly bruised my foot, and it had started to swell. The pain was so great that I skipped my shower. Todd carried my gym bag as I hopped along on one leg for the half-mile walk to my car. I left Todd then and drove myself home.

At home, the pain increased, and my foot was completely blue on top; I thought I had broken something. After agonizing in pain, I decided to go to the hospital emergency room. I drove myself to the hospital and couldn't find a convenient parking space. I got out of the car, and hopped on one leg all the way to the emergency room by myself. Why hadn't my mother or father taken me? Couldn't anyone see that I needed help? Didn't they care? Or were they too busy or distant? The doctor said my foot was only sprained, and many ligaments were torn. It would be at least a few weeks before I could jog again and perhaps never.

At the end of June, both jogging and swimming were stopped indefinitely due to the pain in my foot. Also, my doctor had asked me to stop weight training because my blood pressure was too high. All the exercises that I loved to pursue came to an abrupt end, and there was no other physical outlet for getting rid of stress. I had put in more than a year of hard work to get my body in great shape. I had to let exercise go for a while, and I was disappointed and discouraged because of this.

My body and mind were under high stress because I pushed them to their limits. Being average wasn't good enough; I had to push myself to my limits to be number one. I was a superachiever.

During my teen years, I grew up in a family where there was alcoholism and co-dependency. My parents weren't there for me emotionally much of the time; my father worked and was very busy with his job. I can remember intermittent periods of turmoil and tension in the family. Fights and arguments were common between my parents, and these usually included my younger brother, younger sister, and/or myself. A member of the family began the recovery process from alcoholism, but the rest resisted and remained in denial. As the summer began in 1978, I thought that I didn't have any problems, and I felt immune to the illness that the family had. In reality, I carried tremendous stress, unresolved conflicts, and many "should rules" into the summer of 1978. I didn't know that I had reached my capacity to endure stress, and in 1978 I thought I was invincible and indestructible.

From March through June, I had resumed a friendship with Kim, a girl from my high school days. I felt controlled at times, and this caused a lot of stress and arguments. The more I was around Kim, the more anxiety I had. The thought of becoming close to someone like her scared me. Was she just a friend?

Did I really love her or did I just want to love her? I couldn't figure out what I was feeling, but I knew that I never wanted to feel the pain of rejection in my life. So I resisted and pushed off my involvement with her as much as possible. To feel secure in the relationship, I tried to take control by telling her what behavior and activities were acceptable to me.

To help with all these emotional conflicts, a friend offered to counsel me. He was a psychiatrist at the V.A. Hospital in Durham, North Carolina. Our few conversations never resolved any problems because they only pointed out what I was feeling, not why. After about two months, I stopped seeing Kim because I was overloaded with stress and anxiety. This coincided with the end of June, 1978.

Within the first few days of July, severe depression was rapidly setting in. Life wasn't as sunny as it used to be; darkness rapidly overtook me. I couldn't jog anymore because of my foot injury, and my energy level was getting lower. My zest and enthusiasm in life were decreasing too. Getting to sleep at night took hours as my mind raced for answers. Every day, all day, my head throbbed with pain and pressure. My head felt as if it was being pulled from a vacuum inside. From the moment I woke, to the moment I went to sleep, my body and mind ached with pain. Were there any answers? Who was I? What was my purpose, or the meaning to my existence? I had everything I wanted, but I wasn't satisfied. I knew that I couldn't continue forever in life feeling as bad as I did. Towards the end of July, I made a pact with myself. If I hadn't found my answers by October first, I was going to kill myself. And I meant it! My decision allowed me some peace of mind knowing that my suffering would soon come to an end one way or another.

To seek help for depression and anxiety never occurred to me. I was too independent and thought I could solve all my problems. After all, going to get help for depression would mean that I was mentally ill, and that was in opposition to all that I had worked for—health and a bright mind. Could I really be depressed? I didn't know; I only knew I felt like I was fading fast.

Instead of seeing life as sunny, I saw it as darkness. I identified with the night as I became more depressed. I stayed out until 2 a.m. or 3 a.m. often. I enjoyed the cloudy days, especially the ones with thunderstorms. The gray days were "like" me too; I felt like all colors in life were muted and shaded.

In July, I dropped all my other friends except Todd. I just stopped calling them. When they called me, I told them that I didn't feel well and couldn't go out. I felt too embarrassed to tell them I was "down," and I had lost interest in the activities that my friends and I had in common.

At times, I would imagine that evil and danger were stalking me. Perhaps it was my imagination on fire, but these beliefs and feelings seemed real. When I was returning home one night about 1 a.m., I turned on the radio. I was shocked when instantly the song being played said that I would come to know the devil before the night was through. I was troubled. Was this a warning that when the darkness in my life was full, I would die? And isn't that exactly what I had planned for October first?

From then on, on my way home late at night, the same warning played the instant I turned the radio on. That message wasn't the only thing that scared me on the way home. I was filled with terror at the thought of something evil in the back seat of the car. I didn't feel alone. Fear overwhelmed me so much that I couldn't turn around and look for fear of what I might see—something evil, dark, powerful, and dangerous. Were these the thoughts and emotions of a straight-A, logical, engineering student? What was going on?

As August progressed, my return trips home were approaching 4 a.m., less than two hours until sunrise. I feared that if I stayed out much longer, I would die of this darkness. There may have been other songs on the radio too, but I focused on the ones that had disaster and doom in them. This was typical of my depression, I could see only negative, dark messages. Nothing else registered in my mind.

Summer school had finished in early August, and I had once again made A's for my two courses. I don't know how I got A's in my courses that summer, but I put all my energy into them because the rest of my life felt dead. I remember going to classes and not relating to friends. I was like a zombie—present in body but not in mind or spirit.

The desperation for an answer to my life kept increasing. I had to reach out to someone for help. I was sinking. I was losing. To me, life was like a bumpy road that I was travelling. It was coming to an end, but I couldn't just stop. Where would I go? Who could be trusted? Who would understand?

After telling my mother about my depression and the things I was going through, she said she loved me and that it was hard to understand how I felt. She, as others, said that life wasn't all that bad, and for me to "pick myself up" and get on with living. If I could have changed the way I felt, I would have. Did people really think I chose being depressed?

In August, my family had planned to go on vacation to the beach near Nags Head, North Carolina. Desperately, I wanted time to think. I was like a trapped animal who wanted to be free from misery, and I had the image of falling down a crowded, narrowing, black tunnel. Where do I go when I come to the end? Now I had time just to get away and to search myself for some answers. I was going to have some free time alone.

The several days at the beach were filled with troubled thoughts, and I never really enjoyed myself. I didn't know what I wanted out of my life. I had no purpose in my dead existence, and I couldn't see a clear path for my future. Life seemed lonely and a waste. One evening, I went for a walk on the moonlit beach by myself, and there was no one else out that I could see. Walking through the sea oats, I trudged through the cool fine sand to a point near the beach side of the dunes. I placed my beach towel down on the sand and sat down to do some serious thinking.

The ocean was like a giant endless lake of black oil that slowly and methodically pounded onto the beach one wave at a time. A brilliant full white moon had risen about an hour or two previously; the moon was very white— unusual for the summer. The moon's rays flashed off the ocean as radiant slivers of pure light. Most people would have said it was a beautiful sight, but all I saw was a lonely dark ocean.

But why, with all this beauty, did I feel like I was dying inside? I glanced up and the symbolism of the surroundings overwhelmed me. On the moon was a clear image of a man's face, the "man in the moon." I was excited because the moon represented God to me, and the ocean's darkness was like my life. The moon's brightness represented God trying to shine across the darkness of my life to reach me. The sea was full of life, my life, and it was extremely dark. Yet this brightness was shining a clear pure path right across it. Wherever I went on the beach, the moon's light (or God's light) made a straight path to me. I couldn't escape it. Wow! This was God trying to show me that He was missing from my life. I experienced a truly incredible revelation!

I had believed in God already, yet this incident on the beach clearly pointed out that I had not considered Him in any way as part of the solution to my dilemma. (In August, I didn't recognize that believing God exists and having faith or trust in Him are two different things.) From then on, I knew my answer was tied up in God. But how do I get in touch with someone like that? I didn't know, and my depression only deepened.

After the beach trip, Todd and I were in my house talking, and we kept hearing strange noises in parts of the house; things seemed to be falling over every few minutes. Now and then, a door would shut in a far away bedroom; at least it sounded like it. My fear and anxiety were becoming unmanageable as I saw danger and evil in almost everything. I had to get away from there. Todd and I took off out the door and drove away in his car. We went for a two-hour drive while we both tried to make sense out of my fears and the house's noise. Around 10 p.m. we returned, and whatever made the disturbances was gone. The house was quiet. I felt at ease but still lost and depressed.

In the next two weeks, I returned to work as a co-op student engineer. One of the first duties was to assist in a wood pole test outside in the middle of a sticky tobacco field. The end of summer was oppressive, and the 95° humid heat was more than anyone should have to work in. Yet I felt so dead inside that I didn't care. The sun made me feel that I was being cooked, and I couldn't take it any more.

A doctor said that I had mononucleosis, and my fever was 101°. No wonder I felt so bad! He told me to rest and not go outside in the heat. I took off work for a day or so to recover from the worst of the illness. But actually, it was to last for several weeks as a low-grade tiredness. I don't think the doctor diagnosed me correctly. I think that I had the flu, and the long-term tiredness was from depression.

I still wanted to get away from everyone to have time to think. As always, my thinking went around in circles, and I excluded everyone's input that could have provided an answer. I was always tired, and my sleep was restless. Headaches and a feeling of dark grayness persisted during my waking hours. I couldn't walk normally or smoothly; I sort of mildly staggered and sometimes stumbled. Most everyone thought I was doing fine from outside appearances, but my insides were dying.

Several times in mid-September my mind went blank. My "brain" was ceasing to work, and it was just plain worn out. For several minutes at a time, I didn't even have a thought or feeling.

The poplar trees were turning yellow, and this was the first sign of autumn. This season was a time for things to die out. On September 23, 1978, Todd and I met for the last time at Umstead State Park and went for a walk. I told him that I could no longer be his friend, and that I didn't want to spend time with him again. Todd was the last friend I had, and he was the one I held onto up until the last. He was very distressed at this news and had not correctly judged the level of my discomfort and depression. For that matter, no one really knew how badly I felt. I don't think I knew how to express or describe the pain. Perhaps I was too embarrassed.

The deadline or suicide date had come a week early. I was miserable and had just given up the last friend in my life. I couldn't find even a small reason for living. The pain of depression was all I felt, and it was my driving force. My mind had died. I sat on the couch in the living room and was in turmoil as I started my suicide plans. I had planned to shoot myself, but the gun that I had wanted to use to kill myself was locked up that day. I was so useless that I couldn't even carry through with suicide. At that moment, I was utterly helpless and despondent and at the end of myself. Truly, it is always darkest before the dawn.

Seconds later, a question or thought occurred to me. If I kill myself, will I be jumping off the rim of a hot frying pan into a raging fire? Could it really be worse after death than it was in life? I didn't want to take a chance, and I didn't think of suicide anymore.

Immediately, I thought of my moonlit experience at the beach and other events of the summer. Could I give faith a chance? What did I have to lose? It was then that I said that God had to be real because He was the only "thing" left to try. I asked Him to straighten out the mess my life had become. I turned my life and my will over to Him and asked His help to end my depression.

The next day, as I looked out the window and saw the golden sunrise, I was without the headaches and the inner turmoil. I felt as if that same morning sun had been put inside me along with the newness of the morning. There was no more feeling of darkness, and my "insides" were filled with brilliant light. My deep depression had completely ended overnight. The light at the end of the tunnel was full ablaze, and the dark tunnel had vanished.

I soon began to see my friends again, and they were the ones who stuck by me. My exercise routine picked up, but I never reached even a third of what I had before. I was still a little slow and got tired easily, but the familiar heavy, overwhelming feeling of despair was no more.

I discovered that God loved me and cared deeply about the details of my life, and He accepted me at the worst point in my life. He saw beyond the symptoms of the illness and fell in love with me even before I loved myself. God did not accuse me or pick on me; rather, He was gently guiding me through depression towards Him. He was right there with me in the middle of my depressive symptoms, and He used the depression to reach me. He knew that if I didn't develop a strong faith, I would not make it through even more severe depressions spread over the next nine and a half years! At the end of my road when I knew God was all I had, it was then that I realized He was all I needed.

Did my depression end spontaneously overnight, or did my new faith have something to do with it? I don't know for sure. But from that day on, I always could count on God to help me through the dark times because I associated Him with deliverance from depression.

Bryan L. Court

FOOTPRINTS

One night a man had a dream. He dreamed he was walking along the beach with the LORD. Across the sky flashed scenes from his life. For each scene, he noticed two sets of footprints in the sand; one belonging to him, and the other to the LORD.

When the last scene of his life flashed before him, he looked back at the footprints in the sand. He noticed that many times along the path of his life there was only one set of footprints. He also noticed that it happened at the very lowest and saddest times in his life.

This really bothered him and he questioned the LORD about it. "LORD, you said that once I decided to follow you, you'd walk with me all the way. But I have noticed that during the most troublesome times in my life, there is only one set of footprints. I don't understand why when I needed you most you would leave me."

The LORD replied, "My precious, precious child, I love you and I would never leave you. During your times of trial and suffering, when you see only one set of footprints, it was then that I carried you."

Author Unknown

REFERENCES

American Psychiatric Association. (1994). *Diagnostic and statistical manual of mental disorders* (4th ed.). Washington, DC: Author.

American Psychiatric Association. (1994, December). Practice guidelines for the treatment of patients with bipolar disorder. *The American Journal of Psychiatry, 151*(12), 1–36. Washington, DC: American Psychiatric Press.

American Psychiatric Association, Hospital and Community Psychiatry Service. (1988). *Rights of the mentally disabled, Statements and standards* (rev. ed.). Washington, DC: Author.

Bernstein, J. G. (1988). *Handbook of drug therapy in psychiatry* (2nd ed.). Littleton, MA: PSG Publishing.

Bohn, J., & Jefferson, J. W. (1990). *Lithium and manic-depression: A guide* (rev. ed.). Madison, WI: Lithium Information Center, University of Wisconsin.

Burns, D. D. (1980). *Feeling good: The new mood therapy*. New York, NY: Avon Books.

Burns, D. D. (1993). *Ten days to self-esteem*. New York, NY: William Morrow and Company.

Goodwin, F. K., & Jamison, K. R. (1990). *Manic-depressive illness*. New York, NY: Oxford University Press.

Jefferson, J. W., Greist, J. H., Ackerman, D. L., & Carroll, J. A. (1987). *Lithium encyclopedia for clinical practice* (2nd ed.). Washington, DC: American Psychiatric Press.

Kaplan, H. I., & Sadock, B. J. (Eds.). (1985). *Comprehensive textbook of psychiatry/IV* (4th ed.). Baltimore, MD: Williams & Wilkins.

Loeb, S. (Ed.). (1993). *Physician's drug handbook* (5th ed.). Springhouse, PA: Springhouse Corporation.

Mallory, L. (1984). *Leading self-help groups.* Milwaukee, WI: Family Service America.

Murphey, C. B. (1989). *Breaking the silence: Spiritual help when someone you love is mentally ill.* Louisville, KY: Westminster/John Knox Press.

National Depressive and Manic-Depressive Association. (1991, October). *In bipolar illness: Rapid cycling & its treatment* (brochure). Chicago, IL: Author.

National Depressive and Manic-Depressive Association. (1992, March). *Suicide and depressive illness* (brochure). Chicago, IL: Author.

National Depressive and Manic-Depressive Association. (1993, July). *When treatments fail* (brochure). Chicago, IL: Author.

U.S. Department of Health and Human Services, Health Care Financing Administration. (1993). *Medicare Q&A: 85 commonly asked questions* (rev. ed.) (Brochure). (HCFA Publication No. 02172). Washington, DC: U.S. Government Printing Office.

U.S. Department of Health and Human Services, Social Security Administration. (1992, January). *Disability* (brochure). (SSA Publication No. 05-10029). Washington, DC: U.S. Government Printing Office.

U.S. Department of Health and Human Services, Social Security Administration. (1991, October). *SSI: Supplemental Security Income* (brochure). (SSA Publication No. 05-11000). Washington, DC: U.S. Government Printing Office.

U.S. Department of Health and Human Services, Social Security Administration. (1992, January). *When you get social security disability benefits: What you need to know* (brochure). (SSA Publication No. 05-10153). Washington, DC: U.S. Government Printing Office.

Wrobleski, A. (1989). *Suicide: Why? 85 questions and answers about suicide.* Minneapolis, MN: Afterwards.

Yudofsky, S., Hales, R. E., & Ferguson, T. (1991). *What you need to know about psychiatric drugs.* New York, NY: Grove Press.

INDEX

Note: This index is by question number and/or psychiatrist's response number. "Q" stands for Question Number throughout this book; "PR" stands for A Psychiatrist's Response (or Addition).

MORE QUESTIONS?

If you have additional questions that you would like to see answered in a future edition of this book, please send them to the publisher at the address below and mention the title of this book.

ACCELERATED DEVELOPMENT
A member of the Taylor & Francis Group
3812 West Kilgore Avenue
Muncie, IN 47304-4811
Phone (317) 284-7511; FAX (317) 284-2535

ABOUT THE AUTHORS

Bryan L. Court has spent the majority of his career in civil engineering since graduating *summa cum laude* with a B.S. in civil engineering from North Carolina State University in 1980. Concurrent with his career, he used a great deal of time, effort, and energy in the search for a solution to his own bipolar disorder that began in 1978. During this long process, he attended 12-step groups, mental health support groups, and religious educational activities, and sought help from psychiatrists in an effort to obtain mental health. Without a clear map to recovery, Bryan charted his own way on the difficult recovery journey, and in the process, he learned much about what works and what does not. With his bipolar disorder under control since 1988, Bryan has helped teenagers and adults find their solutions to emotional struggles by passing on his knowledge and experience through volunteer efforts and by writing *Bipolar Puzzle Solution* with Dr. Nelson. Bryan lives in La Jolla, California.

Gerald E. Nelson, M.D., is a board certified psychiatrist with over 20 years experience in child, adult, and family psychiatry and is currently in private practice in Del Mar, California. Nelson is a member of the clinical staff of the University of California Medical School at San Diego. He is author of numerous articles and books including *The One Minute Scolding,* 1984, Shambhala Press (over 70,000 copies sold) and co-author of *Who's the Boss,* 1985, Shambhala Press.